THE 8 SECRETS OF HAPPINESS

Copyright © 2009 Paul Griffiths and Martin Robinson
This edition copyright © 2009 Lion Hudson

The author asserts the moral right
to be identified as the author of this work

A Lion Book
an imprint of
Lion Hudson plc
Wilkinson House, Jordan Hill Road,
Oxford OX2 8DR, England
www.lionhudson.com
ISBN 978 0 7459 5239 8 (UK)
ISBN 978 0 8254 7905 2 (US)

Distributed by:
UK: Marston Book Services, PO Box 269, Abingdon, Oxon, OX14 4YN
USA: Trafalgar Square Publishing, 814 N. Franklin Street, Chicago, IL 60610
USA: Christian Market: Kregel Publications, PO Box 2607, Grand Rapids,
Michigan 49501

First edition 2008
10 9 8 7 6 5 4 3 2 1 0

The text paper used in this book has been made from wood
independently certified as having come from sustainable forests.

A catalogue record for this book is available from the British Library

Typeset in 10/13 ITC Stone Serif
Printed and bound in Great Britain by CPI Cox & Wyman, Reading.

THE 8 SECRETS OF HAPPINESS

PAUL GRIFFITHS & MARTIN ROBINSON

LION

*This book is dedicated to all those who want
to wake up happy.*

Contents

Acknowledgments

There are a host of people who have helped make this book a reality, and have shared their ideas and insights with us. To one and all we want to say thank you.

We particularly want to thank Sharon Lanfear for her help in earthing our comments and offering illustrations of what we were trying to say. Her willingness to read and re-read chapters and offer suggestions has made this book all the better for her input.

We are indebted to the writings of Martin Seligman and other psychologists who have blazed an exciting trail into our understanding of happiness, and to the insightful comments of spiritual gurus of long ago, whose wisdom still speaks today.

This book would also not be a reality without the help of several others: Morag Reeve for believing in the project, Kate Kirkpatrick and Miranda Powell from Lion Hudson for bringing their skills and energy to this exciting adventure and Julie Kite for offering encouragement and advice during the final stages.

Above all, we want to say thank you to our wives and families for their part in our personal happiness and for giving us the time to work on this book.

Introduction

Is it possible to be deeply happy, to have a depth of happiness that sparkles in the routine of everyday life and which overflows even in life's most difficult circumstances and darkest moments?

In *The Road Less Travelled*, bestselling author M. Scott Peck focuses on his conviction concerning one of the greatest truths about life. He faces us with the core reality that life is difficult. He then goes on to argue that many people attempt to avoid this reality. Others, though, do want to know whether there is a quality of happiness that we can access as we face up to, live in and live with the realities of life – a happiness ride which lasts longer than the occasional four minutes on a rollercoaster.

Historians tell us that humankind has always searched for happiness. Plato studied the good life in his academy, Aristotle set up his own college to look at what human flourishing would mean. Over time, Buddha, Confucius, Patnajali and Jesus have all added their insights about this insatiable drive.

Today, this search for the 'blessed life' is expressed in the 56 million hits that the Internet search engine, Google, gets for the word 'happiness' or the fact that there are over 60,000 books in print whose titles are connected with the theme of this earthly nirvana. Recently, *Time* magazine dedicated a special edition to the subject of happiness. It brought together a significant array of research on the subject, most of which was instigated as a consequence of a challenge issued to the American Psychological Association, by their incoming president in 1998. In his presidential speech he noted that throughout its history, psychology had been preoccupied with the idea of making people less miserable (taking them from –5 to 0, as he puts it). He proposed that psychology should actually change its emphasis towards a quest for happiness (taking people from 0 to +5).

From this challenge flowed a large number of studies that all approached different dimensions of the question of happiness. *Time* magazine brought these various studies together and summarized their findings. They wanted to explore and answer the basic question, 'What is it that makes people happy?'

It appears that very few people today report that they are happy. An opinion poll by GfK NOP identified that only thirty-six per cent of the UK population consider themselves to be very happy. Interestingly, along with those conducted in the USA, this poll identified a downward trend in the nation's happiness. Believe it or not, we describe ourselves as more miserable than our parents did at an equivalent time in their lives.

So why is the pursuit of happiness so central to our concerns? Why do we feel that our lives are miserable? And how do we understand the happiness that we seek?

What is happiness?

When it comes to defining happiness, most people are at a loss for words. A major reason for this is that the concept is so difficult to pin down. Money and material possessions are often associated with the attainment of happiness, but describing what happiness would look and feel like is much more tough.

Our western concept of happiness can be traced back to the Greek word *eudaimonia*, which consists of the words *eu* which means 'good' or 'well-being', and *daimon*, meaning 'spirit' or 'one's lot in life'. The problem comes when we attempt to flesh out what that may mean in our modern daily lives.

If nothing else, such ambiguity, as Henri Bergson comments, means that 'each individual may interpret it in their own way'. The capacity for personal choice is highly valued in our individual and multi-optioned society. So, happiness can be as varied as a holiday, a new car or doing better than you thought you would in your annual appraisal. It is something that is pleasing, involves the emotions and can be understood as a passing or momentary experience. In fact, our English word 'happy' derives from the middle English word *hap*, which relates to the idea of happenstance or good fortune.

Many studies have emanated from a range of different disciplines, and thus more formal definitions of happiness have been attempted. However, because of the complexity of the subject, it quickly becomes obvious that no common agreement exists.

In the laboratory of biology, happiness can be defined as that which occurs when a human being connects with the brain's pleasure centre. By contrast, in the debating chamber of politics, politicians are aware that what keeps voters happy is the feeling that the economy is doing well so that people feel prosperous and confident about their future prospects.

While on the couch of psychology happiness may be associated with teaching people to see the glass half full as opposed to half empty, at the popular level it is about 'learned optimism'. You can only be as happy as you decide to be. This is quite different from what is seen in the estate agent's window where happiness is advertised as the possibility of buying a house in the Forest of Dean area. In a recent poll the Forest of Dean was voted one of the happiest places to live in the UK.

Advertisers would have us believe that designer label consumption or commitment to particular brands will bring happiness to our lives. The list of definitions becomes almost endless as we think about the various perspectives offered by employers, friends, family or even those who may want to offer counselling of various kinds.

Clearly these are particular or partial views of happiness. A more substantial view of the nature of happiness can be accessed by considering what we may call the wisdom of the ages in relation to happiness. The eastern tradition, for example, says that all of us are filled with inappropriate desires and that as we rid ourselves of these so we begin to discover happiness. Thus, according to this tradition our failure to obtain happiness does not relate to our absence of material possessions but to our desire to have them in the first place.

Then there is the tradition explored by mystics in both the East and West – the ecstatic tradition. This tradition explores how it is in union with a divine being that we find happiness. Life, then, should be a continual search for transcendent experiences.

Since the nineteenth century, the western tradition – which has generally placed more value on the material world – has tended to suggest that precisely because we are material beings, happiness lies, not in spiritual experiences of one kind or another, but in the very practical and attainable areas of health and wealth.

A more recent refinement of that 'health and wealth' tradition recognizes that we do have other needs and it has developed a range of self-realization theories which suggests that true happiness is found in discovering one's true self and destiny. That does not necessarily mean an obsession with oneself; it could possibly mean getting involved in a cause of some kind – a cause greater than oneself. There are many people today who, for example, find meaning in speaking up for the marginalized in our society or campaigning for a better environment.

So is there some way we can navigate these various views of East and West, of ancient and modern? We can find a clue to such an approach as we look at an older western tradition which comes to us from the ancient world of both the Greeks and Christian mystics and thinkers. This older tradition brings balance by claiming that we are spiritual beings living in a material world. The spiritual is affirmed but the physical is not rejected – it too has a part to play. The suggestion is that when both come together in appropriate ways, we can discover the happy life. It is not just about focusing on the spiritual side of who we are, nor about focusing purely on the physical side of our make-up, but rather by combining both in healthy ways that we are enabled to discover the kind of life that is deeply fulfilling.

In such an approach, dancing with happiness is more a consequence than a purpose. It is more a perpetual state than a momentary emotion. It is more about how you live than what you have. And it is more about what is happening on the inside than how we present ourselves at the superficial level. Because happiness includes our emotions: it involves our intellect or mind; it connects to particular activities, but it also intersects with the spiritual. Happiness is therefore not the goal so much as the outcome of particular ways of living. These ways of living enable us to connect the physical with the spiritual in creative, life-enhancing ways.

What makes people happy?

Some time ago in the UK, the BBC ran a series of features on the science of happiness in which they asked the question 'Is there a formula for happiness?' It doesn't take long when scanning the book titles in the 'Mind, Body and Soul' section of any good bookstore to discover that there is a wide variety of proposed formulas for happiness. Out there in the market place where one size does not fit all, there seems to be hundreds of formulas for happiness, some of which seem very superficial and are certainly untested. Happy to experiment with their own formula, some individuals have a selection box for happiness that can sometimes be shocking and a little too physical for others. In the business of happiness, there is sometimes a difference between imagined longings and researched reality.

The question has been asked for millennia, with the ancient Greeks offering many schools of thought. Socrates advocated self-knowledge as the path to happiness. Plato's 'The Allegory of the Cave' influenced many western thinkers to believe that happiness is found by taking scholarly advice. Aristotle believed that happiness is constituted by moderate, rational activity in accordance with virtue over taking scholarly advice. The Epicureans believed in reaching happiness through the enjoyment of simple pleasures. The Stoics meanwhile believed they could remain happy by being objective and reasonable.

Circumstances...

For those who equate happiness with the presence of favourable circumstances, their shopping list consists of items that aid personal fulfilment. Therefore, happiness is to do with how our career is going, the depth of our relationships, the state of our health, the intensity and frequency of our sex life or the quality of the food we eat. It is about our lifestyle and all of the parts that make it so.

A fairly universal finding from research suggests that beyond a certain point, there is almost no relationship between money (or material possessions) and happiness and yet, when interviewed, most people living in the western world strongly associate money with happiness. However, as economist Richard Layard states, the relationship between our perceived wealth and our perceived happiness is complex. For example, richer nations do not report any greater degree of happiness than poorer nations. When whole societies become wealthier, the degree of happiness reported by the poorest groups and by the wealthiest groups in that society does not change with increases in wealth. The only significant reported shift in happiness ratios is accompanied by a perception of a greater fairness or equality in society. Such a shift is connected to values, ethics and spirituality.

For others, for those who have accomplished many of their personal goals, there comes the surprising discovery that such an achievement does not necessarily lead to the happiness they seek. John McEnroe tells the story of how, having reached the pinnacle of his tennis career, he did not feel that it led to the contentment and happiness that he had anticipated. For McEnroe and for others, the quality of relationships that they enjoyed became much more important.

Back to nature...

Since the 1960s there has been a renewed regard for the environment and a more positive evaluation of nature. Some people have wanted to live simpler lives that are more in tune with nature. One example of this is that of the many hundreds of people from all over the world, who have spent time living at the Findhorn community in north east Scotland. It is here that they have attempted to reconnect with nature in terms of both healing and happiness.

Positive psychology_

As we have mentioned, the recent rise of interest in happiness seems to flow from a challenge thrown out to psychologists to take the issue of happiness more seriously. The results have been fascinating in that popular perceptions of what brings happiness (for example, material wealth) cannot be substantiated by hard research. Actual research suggests that the softer issues, relating more to the spiritual dimension of life, turn out to be at least as important if not more important than the material factors.

Spirituality_

Knowing how to connect the material with the spiritual is a crucial element in the happiness stakes. Yet a review of web pages dealing with happiness reveals that few, if any, mention those vital spiritual factors. The BBC, in an attempt to kick-start the debate on what should be in our happiness formula, mentioned the need for personal meaning and within that implied the necessity of connecting with something outside of oneself. Oliver James, a British psychologist, points out that religious people are much less likely to have what he calls 'virus goals or motivations'. He connects the capacity to live without affluenza (the sluggish, unfulfilled and envious feelings that affect many in the twenty-first century) and the happiness its absence brings, with deeper spiritual values. This is explored further on page 26.

How does the spiritual relate to being happy?

For an increasing minority, there is a growing awareness that happiness and spiritual discovery are deeply connected. So how may we approach happiness from the perspective of spirituality? Just as importantly, what do we mean by spirituality in such a context?

In recent times, those who have an interest in the health of the workplace have been drawn to the relevance of spirituality. This is reflected in the science of management theory where there is enormous growth in the study of spirituality in the workplace.

In today's world, business gurus and trainers talk about a manager's SQ – their spiritual intelligence quotient. This is something that, when combined with EQ (emotional intelligence) and IQ, has the potential to create great leaders. This is because in becoming more aware of who they are and what makes them tick, these influencers are able to focus on developing deeper and more significant aspects of their being.

As we have already suggested, the spiritual dimension to life is embedded in the Greek word for happiness and the aim of this book is to look at the connection between spirituality and happiness. This book is not merely about creating some light relief during a tough afternoon at work – welcome as that may be – but rather, is concerned to develop the presence of happiness that helps to put long-term joy into life and also builds sufficient resilience that we may better face up to life's hardest journeys. To recall the words of the writer M. Scott Peck, life is difficult but those difficulties can be overcome in rewarding ways.

In drawing our understanding of who we are from an older western tradition that recognizes us as spiritual people in a material world, we are going to look at how the spiritual dimension to life, when connected with our daily living, provides a source for deeper happiness. In other words, how do we connect the 'me' that we feel ourselves to be – which is more than just the sum total of our physical attributes – with the physicality of our daily life?

The spiritual dimension that people are increasingly becoming aware of is suggested in the discovery that seven out of ten people pray on a regular basis. Surprisingly, research reports that one of the most frequently asked questions on the part of those outside of any formal religious structures is 'What is the spiritual realm and how does it impact my life?'

Is it still possible to be happy when life is difficult?

Happiness is not dependent on favourable outward circumstances alone. For many people today, life is difficult – not all of the time but certainly for some of it. We may not see our lives as obvious material for the writing of a tragedy, but most of us have experienced sadness of some kind. The deeper happiness this book seeks to describe does not remove all sadness, but rather emphasizes that deeper happiness *can* be found in those who outwardly do not have many reasons to smile.

And so to the chapters...

The search for happiness runs deep in contemporary society. Many magazines run articles on happiness and aging, happiness and your weight, happiness and your heart, even happiness and your kitchen. For many people it has become the Holy Grail – the cup that offers us quality, if not eternal, life. So how do we make sense of so much material? How do we chart a course that can give us some practical direction in the midst of so much data?

Our intention in the following chapters is to help you answer these questions. In order to do so, we shall unpack the findings of the research conducted by writers and thinkers and then published, as aforementioned, by *Time* magazine. The findings were summarized under eight major headings. We will take you through each of these and reveal the golden thread which runs through them all – that there is a spiritual side of humanity which cannot be overlooked in the pursuit of happiness.

Chapter 1

Count your blessings

Introduction

The first question that we want to explore is 'What is the relationship between being thankful and being happy?'

Research conducted by two psychologists, Michael McCullough and Robert Emmons,[1] set out to explore the relationship between happiness and gratitude. Building on the earlier work of Martin Seligman and others who helped to develop the new discipline of positive psychology, McCullough and Emmons performed a series of experiments exploring the links between well-being and the counting of blessings.

In one of these experiments, they invited just over a hundred people to keep a personal journal for ten weeks. Those involved were divided into three groups, each with distinct instructions. The first group were asked to keep a simple record of the events of each day. A second group received directions to catalogue whatever happened during the day that they felt was unpleasant. The last group were invited to list the things from each day that they were thankful for.

At the end of the ten weeks McCullough and Emmons

1 See http://www.acfnewsource.org/religion/gratitude_theory.html.

noted that the level of well-being in the third group who were recording things to be thankful for was generally higher than that of the other two groups. On one level we don't need someone to conduct an experiment to convey that information. A good dose of common sense informs us that if you spend your time thinking upbeat thoughts there will be positive results. However, what these and other psychologists have done for us is to help us appreciate the scientific rationale and ingredients in this formula – and they were even able to measure the impact.

Emmons notes that the practice of such gratitude exercises can increase our happiness level by around twenty-five per cent. How does being grateful make you happier? Well, it is related to extracting more pleasure out of the life that we have. As singer Sheryl Crow puts it, 'It's not getting what you want, but wanting what you've got.'

Seligman's research suggests that there are three components that can raise your happiness level. First, you need to find ways of making your life more meaningful. Second, it is important to become more engaged in what you do. Third, you need to work at getting more pleasure out of your life. This last part includes savouring the experiences that you go through and learning to savour what you have (see chapter 3).

What does it mean to count your blessings?

Very simply, counting your blessings involves taking the time to appreciate all that you have. It means creating opportunities to consider how fortunate you are. It could be described as cataloguing the many treasures that you possess or opening your life wardrobe and admiring your collection. It clearly includes opening your eyes to the many gifts that everyday life presents.

In the film *The Colour of Paradise*, Iranian director and screenwriter Majid Majidi introduces us to Mohammad, a delightful and sensitive eight-year-old blind boy who every summer excitedly leaves the Blind Institute in Tehran in order to spend his holiday at home with his father and grandmother. Enhanced by his inability to physically see, Mohammad has developed the capacity to look at life through the eyes of his heart. As someone who is filled with life, he is continually exploring that which is going on around him.

Mohammad is treasured by his grandmother, but not by his father. During a summer that should have seen Mohammad flourishing in the countryside around his home he is sadly taken away and placed as an apprentice to a blind carpenter. With his arranged marriage fast approaching, Mohammad's father sees his son as an obstacle and is keen therefore to offload him as quickly as possible.

Despite being the father of a child who is caught up in the awe and wonder of that which surrounds him, Mohammad's father is a man who cannot see the treasure in front of his own eyes.

To count our blessings we must learn to open our eyes to the beauty that surrounds us – as G. K. Chesterton said, we need to 'get into the habit of taking things with gratitude and not taking things for granted'. As we shall discover later, this is no easy feat. Eric Hoffer once said that 'the hardest arithmetic to master is that which enables us to count our blessings'. And yet, the pursuit of this quality is important because it enables us to celebrate the sacred in the ordinary of each day.

A grateful heart

The idea of counting your blessings is part of a bigger recipe for happiness. Counting your blessings suggests some attitudinal changes which we may describe as the development of a grateful heart. In turn, the development of a grateful heart is a way of life, a mindset or a salsa beat that causes us to find deep appreciation for the good things that we see and experience. It is the recognition of abundance, the acknowledgment of blessing.

There is a discussion to be had as to what comes first – counting your blessings or a grateful heart. It is best however to see them as feeding each other – with the option of beginning at either point. It is clear that from a heart of gratitude comes a fresh perspective that enables us to see many of the blessings around us. And the more ways we find to give thanks, the more things we will find to be grateful for. As one Nigerian saying goes, 'Give thanks for a little and you will find a lot.'

Our fascination with gratitude is not something new. From earliest times spiritual and philosophical thinkers have celebrated gratitude. Most of the world's major religions, be they Judaism, Christianity, Islam or Hinduism, prize gratitude. Not only is it a beneficial emotional state and not only does it encourage a reciprocal kindness, but for some it is also a mirroring of the divine nature.

As already noted, we need to see ourselves as spiritual beings in a material world. Gratitude is one of the key components of a spiritual life and very important if we are to be aware of the sacred moments and significance of each day. It could be argued that gratitude is the beacon that makes us aware of a divine friend. As Albert Schweitzer, a man of legendary skills – theologian, musician, philosopher and physician – points out, those who have learned to live out of a grateful heart know what it means to truly live, they have penetrated the whole mystery of life.

The power of saying thank you

In her book *Thank You Power: Making the Science of Happiness Work for You*, Deborah Norville talks about the power of being thankful. Following on from her personal reflection about her own life and noting that when she focused on things that were positive she felt better, this prized author went on to research the innate power in saying thank you. Her discovery was that not only did being thankful put people's minds in a more positive place but it also had the possibility of unlocking their full potential – that is, being all that they were created to be.

This is a similar line of thought to Oprah Winfrey's remarks at the beginning of one of her April 2000 TV shows when she said, 'Thank you. Two words that can make miracles.' Such is the power of being thankful that scientists have viewed it as treatment for a whole host of ailments and as an additive with which to colour one's life.

In addition to recording the findings on their experiments, McCullough and Emmons also cited how people who focus on things they are grateful for are happier than those who don't. In addition they noted some of the many other advantages of gratitude. Those who were thankful experienced a better quality of sleep,[2] had more meaningful exercise and were more optimistic about the week ahead. Fewer people reported physical symptoms such as pain. There was also evidence of a greater connection to other people and an intention to help others deal with their own personal problems.

---

2 One of the most interesting links currently being investigated is that of gratitude and insomnia. As one witty article put it, 'Sleepless in Seattle? Then count your blessings.'

These same findings were also picked up in research reported by *Time* magazine editor, Claudia Wallis, who noted that those who engaged in gratitude exercises not only saw their mood lift but were also more likely to have improved physical health, raised energy levels and in situations where there was neuromuscular pain-relief from some of these symptoms.

That is not to suggest that gratitude by itself is a 'cure all' for every condition. In terms of the relationship between thankfulness and depression, researchers are unclear. There is some benefit to be found, but for many people a more effective form of help should be sought. Scientists[3] tell us that those who are grateful are also likely to engage in random acts of kindness to others – it really is contagious.

In experiments conducted at the University of Pennsylvania it was recorded that of the twenty-four signature strengths of character – those which together make a vibrant individual – gratitude, love and hope were in the top three. Gratitude therefore plays a significant role in a person's sense of well-being.

Blessed

So, if we are to count our blessings, what does it mean to be blessed? For those who lived in the days of Plato and Aristotle, to be blessed would have meant to live life with good fortune. It was a term that was used of the gods who prospered and those individuals who were seen as sharing their quality of life here on earth. Those who lived a blessed life were not victims to earthly frailties or misfortunes. According to the Bible, blessedness is a quality of life experienced by those who walk with God and a result of spiritual maturity. According to Jesus in the Sermon on the Mount, the poor in spirit are blessed, by which he meant that they understood their need to depend on God.

So what does it mean to be blessed today? As most people are caught up in the narrative of consumerism, popular definitions include money, possessions, which car you drive, where you live and the size of your bank balance. Unfortunately, in our fast-paced world, the exact details of what should be in our 'must-have carrier bag' are forever changing. Taking the American Dream as an example, in the early 1950s life was all about achieving a three-bedroom suburban house and a good car. It was about Dad going to work and Mom staying at home to look after the children. There was a pleasant pace to life.

Some observers noticed that by the 1980s the American Dream had become a lot more expensive. Now it was necessary for both Dad and Mom to work and for far longer than forty hours a week. Happiness was still in the possession of things.

Today it is all of the above and more.

In his book, *Affluenza*, Oliver James suggests that many today are infected by 'affluenza'. He says that the desire to consume, to have wealth and to keep up with the Joneses constitutes a virus which distorts our view of the world around us. James describes the virus as placing a high value on money, possessions, appearances (physical and social) and fame. Those who have such a virus show evidence of profound emotional distress. James uses his book to give practical examples of those who are living with the virus and offers a number of antidotes. He notices that those who do not have the virus are aware of reasons for being grateful for the good things they do have.

Writing in the same vein, Richard Layard notes the paradox that most people want more income and yet as populations become wealthier, they do not actually become any happier. In some cases they become significantly less happy. As identified in our introduction, the consumer mindset is a fairly recent development and one that many are finding deeply unsatisfying. A worldview that fails to see us as spiritual people living in a material world, is unable to fully understand gratitude. The rush to consume always looks for more of everything and rarely stops for long enough to be thankful for what we already have. Deep within the consumer story lies the suggestion that consuming more will always be better.

And so we return to the question, 'What does it mean to be blessed?' It means to recognize life is full of blessings without the need to consume yet more. Blessings can be material and spiritual; present and future; human and divine; personal and social. They are gifts that fill our lives, some of which can be bought with money and most of which cannot. They include a refreshing cup of tea after a long cold walk and the companionship of a faithful friend during a difficult time. What does it mean to be blessed? It means to be in a place where you are aware of and appreciate the precious gifts of life that have been given to you.

An unknown benefactor

So where do blessings come from and where do you go to say thank you? The realization that we may not be the sole author of all the good things that we have – in other words that we are not entirely self-sufficient – is an important concept in the creation of thankfulness. At one level we may come to see that there are many in our family and among a wider circle of friends who have offered us kindness. Stopping to acknowledge the care we have been given is a good start in the gratitude stakes.

Beyond that, those who have begun to practise an attitude of thankfulness have come to embrace a sense of wonder and awe that flows from an awareness that there are forces in the universe that are far greater than we are. To know that life is more than the material, that there is a spiritual dimension to the world, that we are spiritual beings, is to begin the journey that leads us to see that we are loved.

It's curious that many people find a desire to connect with the divine when overwhelmed by some unexpected and gracious act that has impacted them. Perhaps this is no better illustrated than in how the old hymn 'Amazing Grace' has been used again and again at times of heartfelt gratitude. There was an incident when, one night, late in the twentieth century, a whole community was overwhelmed with such a feeling of thankfulness. People had been divided by war; boundaries had been drawn and strictly enforced. Families and friends had been made to live out of reach of each other. And then, on this fateful night in 1989, the Berlin Wall came down. Those who had once walked together along the same streets were able to do so again. Many sang together in celebration:

Amazing grace, how sweet the sound,
that saved a wretch like me.
I once was lost, but now am found,
was blind but now I see.

In reflecting on what it means to be blessed, it is important to recall the surprising words of physicist Stephen Hawking, who recently expressed that to be blessed was not dependent upon everything in life being perfect. In speaking about his own life he is able to acknowledge how he has learned to count his blessings. He says, 'I don't have much positive to say about motor neurone disease, but it taught me not to pity myself because others were worse off, and to get on with what I still could do. I'm happier now than before I developed the condition.'

Steps to take

When it comes to finding practical ways to count your blessings – be it to say thank you to someone or to engage in an activity that will help you appreciate how blessed you are – then the list is as limitless as one's creativity or time spent surfing the Internet looking for one more idea. Here are some suggestions to get your creativity underway.

Keep a gratitude journal

One of the most popular ways of counting your blessings is to keep a gratitude journal. Although there are numerous gurus suggesting how you should practise such journaling, the overall consensus is that to journal three or four times a week is the ideal for most people.

The idea is that you make a simple list or write about special memories of those things that have happened that day, or since you last journaled, that you consider a blessing. Advocates for the practice of journaling include Oprah Winfrey, psychologists in the field of behavioural psychology and thousands of ordinary people who already engage in journaling on a regular basis.

Writing in her book *Simple Abundance*, author Sarah Ban Breathnach describes journaling as a transformative process. It is something that will cause a shift to occur in your inner reality over a period of a few months. The obvious advantage of a gratitude journal is that it is also a treasure box of stories that you can return to again and again as a reminder of the good things that have happened in your life.

Write a gratitude letter or email

Several years ago, Ron had the privilege of travelling to South Korea to speak at several events across Seoul. This was the farthest that he had ever travelled from home and it was definitely the most exciting opportunity that he had ever been given. It was an incredible adventure – the people organizing the trip had taken time to prepare a great itinerary for him, he was hosted in a beautiful location and every day different people were appointed to act as tour guides during his free time.

He was so moved by the whole experience that before long he found himself thinking about all the people who had been involved in his training and early formation as a communicator. He thought about those who together had shaped him into being the person he now was and therefore indirectly made this trip possible.

Such was his level of gratitude that he found himself writing a series of emails to many people who had invested time, energy and wisdom in him. The act of carefully writing those emails not only deepened his sense of gratitude, but also helped him to express the joy that was his.

Send a thank you card

The communication process can be made easier and become a more regular habit by sending someone a simple card that expresses the joy you have received from their act of kindness. If you enjoy being creative, you could make the card yourself.

Make a gratitude visit

Some people reckon that this is the one to turbocharge your happiness. Rather than send someone a letter, the idea is that you either take the letter and then read it to them, or that you simply visit them and tell them what they mean to you. You can supplement the visit with the physical act of buying a bunch of flowers and/or a bottle of wine as a thank you gift for your friends who have helped you accomplish something that would have been difficult if you had attempted it on your own. A visit to their home to give them a gift and to tell them how much you appreciate them clearly has the potential for tears to flow.

Buy gratitude tokens

When Betty recently returned from a trip of a lifetime where she had been visiting various care projects in Africa, she brought back several souvenirs of her trip. To help her continually recall the sense of wonder that she encountered on her travels, she brought home a bookmark, a small drum and a handmade African dress. The strategic placing of such tokens creates gratitude prompts that will continually remind us of the good days we have experienced. For some, a gratitude token could take the shape of a small flag of the country which has been visited or a piece of pottery or jewellery. It can help to remind them of the privilege they have had of working in and experiencing something of a different people group.

Make a mental gratitude list

Set yourself the mental challenge of coming up with five things you can be thankful for. If it helps, set a prompt on your PDA or Outlook Calendar or in your diary to remind you to repeat the process on a weekly basis.

Learn the ABC of giving thanks

This is similar to the mental gratitude list. Set yourself the goal of coming up with one reason for every letter of the alphabet for how you have been blessed. This is probably best done on a weekly basis and with a piece of paper and a pen!

Say 'grace' more often[3]

There are numerous people who are in the habit of saying 'grace' before a meal. It is a moment in time in which they can express gratitude for the food that has been provided and those who have been involved in getting it ready and serving it. Some suggest that people learn to expand the number of occasions and the settings (don't just associate it with the eating of food) in each day where one says grace. If the saying of grace is an act of marking and expressing gratitude for a good thing that is happening or about to happen, then it could be appropriate to say it before a concert or a day out with family or a visit to the theatre or cinema.[4]

Make a gratitude calendar

This is something that you can do for yourself or with your family or even those you work with. Either purchase or make a simple calendar that gives space for someone to write down something for which they can be thankful every day.

---

3 See the Appendix 1 (page 156) for suggestions for saying grace.
4 One of the most interesting links currently being investigated is that of gratitude and insomnia. As one witty article put it, 'Sleepless in Seattle? Then count your blessings.'

Practise saying thank you more often

Taking the advice of G. K. Chesterton seriously, why not get into the habit of taking things with gratitude and not for granted. Although a simple discipline, verbally articulating our gratitude for something has the potential to enrich many experiences.

Thank you meal

How delightful it is to go out for a meal with friends or family or workmates and to use the occasion as an opportunity to say thank you. The purpose of the event can greatly heighten your sense of gratitude.

Celebrating special days

Our calendars are already filled with opportunities to hold special thank you days. America celebrates 'Thanksgiving' and the UK celebrates 'Harvest Thanksgiving'. Then there are Father's Day and Mother's Day and now Grandparents' Day is emerging. These days afford us the opportunity to stop for a moment and express our gratitude to those who have loved and cared for us.

The giving and receiving of gratitude gifts

Our bookshelves are filled with numerous gifts that we have been given by the various individuals and groups we have worked with. Each has been given to us as an expression of their gratitude. For them and for us the act of giving and receiving of gifts has stirred feelings of gratitude, as do the memories that they produce.

Gratitude song

A practice employed by Oprah Winfrey that expresses and marks her gratitude is that of singing the old religious classic 'Jesus Loves Me'. She sings it every time she runs by her house. It is reported that on one occasion she forgot to sing this song when she jogged past her house and so went back and sang it twice as she ran in front of the gates. It is a similar idea to that portrayed in the amusing American TV series *Ally McBeal*. Based at a law firm, the weird and wonderful characters in this show spent their lives in constant turmoil. They used their gratitude song to re-centre themselves and lift their spirits.

Do the gratitude dance

Without doubt the most amusing way of marking the blessings of life is to learn and then perform the gratitude dance. Posted on the Internet site YouTube, the dance is a simple, crazy and yet potentially significant way of counting one's blessings.

Gratitude for the body?

One of the exercises encouraged by some gratitude gurus is that of taking time to thank each and every part of their body for fulfilling the role that it does.

Learning to count

In thinking through the component parts of how we go about counting our blessings, there has to come a point where we don our Dr Phil McGraw[5] hat and begin to get

---

5 Phil McGraw holds a PhD in clinical psychology. He has appeared on numerous Oprah Winfrey shows and is famous for his 'get real' approach.

real about what this truly means. In pursuing a deeper heart of gratitude and within that the discipline of counting your blessings, there are a number of underlying personal attitudes that have to be explored. Some of these will aid our pursuit of the happy life and some, if left unchecked, will have the potential to rob us of it.

As an aside, it should be noted that there is another way of developing a grateful heart. Many have come through an experience of loss, pain or tragedy with a much clearer sense of gratitude – an awareness that previously they had taken much for granted. If we had a choice, it is clearly not the best route to travel. Author and former British politician, Jeffrey Archer, may be able to say that he is happier as a consequence of lessons learned through his experiences in prison. His downfall caused him to count his blessings. But clearly, there is a better way to count our blessings than to wait for tragedy to befall us. So, what are some of the underlying attitudes that need to be explored?

Contentment

Contentment is sometimes described as the neuro-physiological experience of satisfaction, of being at ease with one's situation. Promoters of yoga might tell us that it is aided by breathing exercises and concentration. Ghandi told us that our 'happiness really lies in contentment'.

The problem is that we live within a society where we are continually being bombarded with messages that encourage us to want more, buy something better and purchase the next or latest version or model of car or ipod. If contentment is anything, then it is the wisdom to know that sometimes enough is enough, that there comes a point when you lose more than you gain in pursuit of yet one more thing. To focus on what we have rather than on what we don't have is the beginning of gratitude.

Having a truer appreciation of the worth of things

Antique collectors may consider it pure bliss to be able to spend an afternoon exploring local antique or second-hand shops in search of that rare piece. Their experience is that quite often such items are undervalued. How easy it is to pick up something for a few pence and then sell it for several hundred pounds on an Internet auction website. In coming to the place of counting our blessings we have to learn how to put the right price tag on the garments that we have in our life wardrobe. The companionship of a friend is a far greater blessing than the latest gadget. Friends who keep their promises are far more precious than the most expensive pair of Jimmy Choo shoes or the rarest diamond from Tiffany's.

Learning to celebrate others

A key to the rearing of children is to help them celebrate the successes of their siblings rather than be envious or undermined by them. This attitude is also important in forming a mindset that allows us to count our blessings. Those who are forever living in the shadow of the 'Joneses' will never be free to enjoy what they already have. The disastrous impact of envy is well illustrated in the film *Amadeus*, which portrays the alleged relationship between Antonio Salieri and Amadeus Mozart. Salieri was court composer to Emperor Joseph II and the toast of all of Vienna and yet such was his jealousy of Mozart that he set about ruining the young composer's life. Unable to celebrate the gift of the other and aware of his own artistic poverty in the light of Mozart's talent, Salieri hatched a scheme that would bring the irreverent composer to harm. Salieri continually tried to thwart Mozart's attempts to advance his career or to have his compositions played. In reality it led to Salieri's own destruction when his claim to having poisoned Mozart was discredited and the attempt to take his own life failed – leaving him to live out the rest of his life in mediocrity.

In all of this, it is important to see gratitude as a muscle that needs to be regularly exercised. The occasional visit to the gym of thankfulness is never going to develop our gratitude muscles to the point where we are in a far better shape. We need to note in our diaries regular times to exercise our new practice of gratitude. It is not easy, but the long-term benefits will be far more enjoyable than just being able to flaunt our toned shape at the gym!

Chapter 2

Practise acts of kindness

Introduction

Recently, the first ever 'Happy List' was published. Published in *The Independent* in April 2008, this was a list that identified a hundred people who have all made the United Kingdom a better and happier place. The noteworthy dimension of this roll of honour was that it celebrated ordinary and unknown individuals as well as those with the 'Midas touch' or those who had celebrity status. These were people who had given of their time or money or energy or creativity to make the UK a brighter place in which to live.

There were those like Tommy Callagher, a milkman who in his spare time had raised over £100,000 for the British Heart Foundation. There were individuals such as John Aldis, who had founded 'Street Angels', a volunteer scheme for Watford town centre which sees teams of caring people going out onto the streets between 9 p.m. and 3 a.m. to help the vulnerable. There were characters like Ade Adepitan, a wheelchair basketball star and TV presenter, who was honoured for having one of the smiliest faces on TV.

In setting themselves the task of identifying a hundred 'Good Samaritans', the compilers of the list cited that their greatest challenge was limiting it to only a hundred names. It seems that acts of kindness are to be found everywhere; reports of random acts of kindness include an incident involving Simon Cowell, *X Factor*'s 'Mr Nasty'. On a recent Oprah Winfrey show, he was moved to give £80,000 ($162,000) to help a family who had been struggling to pay their mortgage since their three-year-old daughter had been diagnosed with a rare form of cancer.

Then there is the story of the Birmingham City soccer player who gave one of the apprentices at the club his hugely expensive Mercedes. The boy had been shadowing Olivier Kapo as part of his training and had hoped – not unrealistically – for a pair of the player's old boots at the end of the season. Kapo's response was to give the trainee his 'run-around' car and also pay for a year's insurance.

It is reported that as well as being a great actor, the late Paul Newman was apparently an incredibly kind man. His obituaries spoke not only of his amazing career but also the way in which he either gave money or raised money for countless worthy causes. He, like the New Zealand eye doctor Fred Holloway and the Australian heart surgeon Victor Chang, spent time expressing kindness to others. Then there are the tens of thousands (if you can put a number on it) of thoughtful deeds enacted by individuals in their everyday lives. Those who speak a kind word, offer a pleasant smile, hold a door open for someone to walk through or help run a local community group.

What does it mean to be kind?

Kindness is one of those traditional virtues that have been highly regarded for centuries. It belongs to those qualities of character such as courage and justice, hope and mercy. Its origin in old English is *gecynde*, which meant 'natural' or 'native'. In Middle English the earliest sense was that of being well-born or well-bred. It implied someone who was by nature courteous, gentle and benevolent.

One of the most dramatic illustrations of such a quality is that exhibited by Jean Valjean, an ex-convict, in *Les Misérables*. If kindness is the quality of being friendly, generous and considerate, then Valjean lives this out in his dealing with Cosette, the daughter of one of his anonymous and insignificant factory workers. Valjean takes responsibility for Cossette in line with the deathbed request of her mother. With a plot located around the time of the French Revolution we see this one man shine out in the darkness of despair that existed at that time. Such is the quality of his self-giving that later in Cosette's life he joins student Marius, the man that Cosette loves, at a doomed barricade. Students have gathered there to fight for freedom and democracy, but against the army they have no chance. Valjean risks his own life by dragging Marius away just before the students are over-run. Then, as he is nearing old age, Valjean makes his greatest sacrifice for Cosette. He gives up his relationship with her so that his long-ago, but not forgotten, indiscretions should not damage her. At Marius and Cosette's wedding, Valjean confesses to Marius the shame and misdeeds of his criminal past. Marius, shocked by the revelations, and wanting to save Cosette from the implications (unaware that it had been Valjean who had rescued him from the barricade), drives Valjean away. Valjean leaves and retires to his deathbed – full of great sadness but willing to do so for the good of Cosette.

The psychologist Martin Seligman lists kindness among twenty-eight character strengths and virtues. For Seligman, kindness includes the dimensions of generosity, nurture, care, compassion and altruistic love (more of that later in the chapter). Elsewhere Seligman comments that it is a quality that can make you happier than the cerebral virtues of curiosity and the love of learning. It is that mindset of preferring others that Jesus encouraged people to pursue when he commented that you should love your neighbour as yourself.

Included in the seven virtues, a list that was set up as a contrast to the seven vices or deadly sins, kindness is specifically set against the vice of envy, the most miserable of all the vices. There may be a degree of fun in the twisted vices of pride or gluttony or lust but in envy there is absolutely no pleasure.

Some have described kindness as the social miracle – the fact that we can care for each other, even be concerned for those we are not directly related to or geographically near. Henry James, the American novelist, said that the three most important things in life are kindness, kindness and kindness.

Kindness as a spiritual quality

The Jewish Talmud claims that 'deeds of kindness are equal in weight to all commandments'. St Paul, a former persecutor of Christianity who became one of its primary spokesmen after a mystical encounter with Jesus, defined deepest love as that which is 'patient and kind'. This is love that is not focused on self but is concerned with the well-being of others.

In Buddhism, *metta*, or loving kindness, is one of the ten virtues that are pursued to obtain the unobstructed life on the way to Enlightenment. Used in meditation, people are encouraged to think kind thoughts about themselves, then their family, then their friends, then enemies and then all of creation. *Metta* meditation is thought by some to aid in the calming down of an angry mind. Tenzin Gyatso, the fourteenth Dalai Lama, said 'My religion is kindness.' Even Confucius urged his followers to 'recompense kindness with kindness'.

Christianity teaches that kindness is connected with: friendliness – encouraging individuals towards lasting relationship; compassion – caring about the needs of others; helpfulness – generous action; forbearance – responding kindly to those who are negative towards you.

To state the obvious, one of the most important areas where there needs to be an epidemic of such kindness is in the home, whether this is in our interactions with our partner or with our children – there is often a shortage of kindness.

We have to discover how to be more understanding, and give more of our time, to ensure that we carry at least our share of the household chores. When we are wronged or feel that we have been, many of us have to develop the capacity not to retaliate. Some of us need to work at becoming friendly again.

In the ancient manuscript of Ecclesiastes, Solomon, a man who seemed to have everything – riches and wisdom – recalls his journey towards a life worth living. Satiated with all the pleasures that this world could offer him he went in search of life's most precious experiences. His conclusion after his full and exhausting search was that life was all about giving yourself away – wholeheartedly. He concluded that being kind to others was one of the most precious experiences of life. Kindness for him was a giving away of yourself to others that included the full use of your mind, will and emotion.

What is more, kindness brings people into contact with the divine. Dr Jonathan Haidt's pioneering work on what happens to those who witness someone else's act of generosity reveals that they experience a sensation he terms 'elevation'. It is a moment when they can experience a sense of awe as they observe that godlike quality in another human being.

Haidt's interest in this topic was awakened by earlier research he did on the phenomenon of disgust. In logging how people reacted to expressions of the darker side of our humanity he began to consider what might be our response to acts of self-giving. For Haidt, the particular area of application for his work was that of the family. In encouraging parents to model such behaviour in the home he hoped to encourage children to do likewise. If nothing else it has the potential to stir hope.

An explosive quality – the miracle drug

Kindness is powerful. Writing in his book, *The Healing Power of Doing Good: The Health and Spiritual Benefits of Helping Others*, Allan Luks notes that the potentially positive effects of being kind to others are:

- a more optimistic and happier outlook on life
- a heightened sense of well-being
- a sense of exhilaration and euphoria
- an increase in energy
- a feeling of being healthy
- decreased feelings of loneliness, depression and helplessness
- a sense of connectedness with others
- a greater sense of calmness and relaxation
- increased longevity

- better weight control

- an improvement in insomnia

- a stronger immune system

- a reduction in pain

- increased body warmth

- a healthier cardiovascular system (reduction in blood pressure, improved circulation, reduced coronary disease)

- a reduction of excessive stomach acid

- a decrease of oxygen requirement

- relief from arthritis and asthma

- speedier recovery from surgery

- reduced cancer activity.

Not only can kindness impact the giver and the receiver, it even has the power to change the world. As Steve Carell's character, Evan, discovered in the film *Evan Almighty*, God used him to change his world taking one small step at a time.

In addition to all these benefits, kindness is a deeply attractive quality for those looking for a partner. In a study of thirty-seven cultures around the world, 16,000 subjects were asked about their most desired trait in a mate. For both sexes, the first preference was kindness.

Kindness has the potential to make people as happy, if not happier, than the people to whom some expression of compassion is made. The 'happy list' is not only a collection of those who have made others happy, it is also a catalogue of those who have become happier themselves.

How being kind makes you happier – the science!

One of the pioneer investigators into the links between kindness and fulfilment is Stanford University psychologist Sonja Lyubomirsky. In one of her experiments she encouraged a group of students in her class to do five random acts of kindness a week for several weeks. As a result, her students reported higher levels of happiness than the control group. What is more, those who completed their five acts of kindness in one day reported even higher levels of happiness.

Lyubomirsky's results are in line with those from a study conducted in Canada about how employees spend their bonuses. This study concluded that those who gave some of their bonuses away to charity had a greater sense of well-being than those who did not. Both these experiments reinforce earlier findings that note how altruistic people tend to be happier people.

When it comes to the specifics of how being kind makes you happier, psychologists say that it is not easy to join the dots. The exact pathways are still to be discovered. For instance, one of the discussions asks whether such a quality of character is to be found in our humanity or in some kind of transcendence.

Apparently, however, we can identify some happiness boosters as a result of the practice of kindness. Some suggest that the reason being kind makes us happy is that it makes us feel generous and capable. As Christopher Peterson argues, it makes us feel good about ourselves. It's like buying yourself a Burberry bag or Plasma HD-ready digital TV.

Others believe that the reason being kind makes us happy is that it gives us a greater sense of connectedness with others. The idea of feeling more connected with those around seems to be the outcome from most experiments conducted by positive psychologists.

45

Then there are those who consider that being kind makes you happy because it wins you approval from others. For some the reason that being kind can make you happier is that it often produces a kinder response in others.

There are a few who think that the reason why being kind helps in putting a smile on your face is that it distracts you from your own existence for a few moments and with that your own needs and wants…

But perhaps one of the loudest explanations given as to how being kind makes us happier is that it brings meaning into our lives. It helps us appreciate that we really matter, and can make a difference.

How being kind makes you happier – part 2

As well as identifying the boosters that stimulate a happier lifestyle, science has also crafted for us a number of accessories that help with our outfit. Sonja Lyubomirsky has identified how those who felt strongly that others appreciated their effort often experienced a bigger happiness boost. It doesn't mean to say that we should only be kind to those who we know will be deeply appreciative, but such knowledge does guard against us feeling too flat after some kind acts.

Jonathan Haidt from the University of Virginia comments on how for significant returns on our gestures of kindness we need to choose deeds that strengthen existing social ties. For him it is about actions such as taking our grandparents out for a drive. He is not advocating that we do not express care randomly or to strangers. Rather, that we focus as much, if not more, attention on those we already have a relationship with.

Further fascinating insights about the relationship between 'loving your neighbour as yourself' and happiness come from two experiments conducted in Japan. Entitled 'Happy people become happier through kindness', psychologists explored the strength of kindness among people who were already happy – a neglected field of research.

Their findings were that happier people are more likely to be kinder people than those who are sad. Apparently, those who spend time thinking carefully about kind deeds become even happier – there is power in the conscious awareness that kindness is being practised. This kind of contemplation about kind deeds produces a positive reinforcing cycle of greater happiness and then even greater kindness.

In considering the place and extent of kindness in our own lives, it is important to think about these questions:

1. How much do I think about kindness?

2. How easy is it to recognize kindness in others?

3. How often do I do acts of kindness?

Cultivating the kindness gene (motivation)

When it comes to identifying where the tendency towards kindness originates, social scientists are divided. This hotly debated issue sees researchers divided into two groups: those who believe in altruism and those who do not.

One tradition, 'universal egoism', suggests that every kind deed is ultimately committed for the benefit of the self. Nothing, it is argued, is done cleanly. There is always the presence of self-benefit. Not that there is anything wrong with that; the argument is pointed solely at the notion of selfless love.

Pillars on which the temple of self-advancement is built include the idea that doing something kind reduces the tension created by our sense of empathy and inaction. We all know what it is like to encounter someone in desperate

47

need and feel that we ought to help. How many of us have offered to help a neighbour for no other reason than we feel we ought to rather than because we want to?

Then there is the notion that a kind act allows us to avoid social sanction or personal guilt for failing to help. There is a great storyline in the seventh series of the US drama *The West Wing* where the White House Chief of Staff is head-hunted to work for an extremely rich person. His offer is that he will give CJ ten billion dollars to go and help the world in some way. His motivation for such a gesture is the belief that it is socially rude not to give some of his exorbitant wealth away.

One other argument presented to oppose the idea of altruism is that kindness confers social and personal rewards. Mockingly termed 'reciprocal altruism' it highlights how kind acts are most often done for those who are likely to repay us in some way. Some people may offer to put their neighbour's bins out when they are away in the hope that the neighbours will look after theirs when they in turn are on holiday. But even this can't apply to all circumstances – think of all the acts of kindness that are done anonymously.

Standing in the opposing corner are those who believe that many kind deeds come from those who have a selfless concern for others. Considered to be the golden rule of ethics and standing in opposition to selfishness, altruism is about more than having a sense of loyalty or duty. It is the attitude whereby a person engages in acts of kindness with no thought of personal gain. It comes from the heart of someone who is generous, compassionate and has a deep sense of the other person's worth.

Imago Dei

In putting forward the idea that some people have this kind of innate goodness within them – a natural bent towards desiring the well-being of others – an important question to ask is 'Where does this internal bias come from?' For those from the older western tradition the belief is that this action of preferring others before ourselves comes from the fact that we are made in the image of God. Although slightly faded from its original condition, our desire and ability to be kind is in our DNA.

One of the questions asked by those interested in spirituality is, 'If there is a God, what is he or she like?' In describing the nature of God in the pages of its sacred text, Christianity offers a picture of a God who is good – a God who is kind and gracious. God is noted as a being who is full of goodwill towards people. He is kind to his creation, to all people, to those who follow him and to those who do not. Therefore we act selflessly because to some extent we share the nature of God.

If we do bear some traces of the image of God then how can we develop that positive element? Ebenezer Scrooge in Charles Dickens's *A Christmas Carol* might have needed three ghosts to lead him to the place of appreciating the joy of being kind. Fashion advisors attempt to help people change their external wardrobe and dress. But how do we cultivate the kindness, or *imago dei* (image of God), that is in us?

What stops us from being kind and how do we overcome this?

Of all the obstacles to overcome in the exercise of random acts of kindness perhaps the most challenging is that of envy. Often associated with the colour green as in 'green-eyed monster' or 'green with envy' or 'seeing green', envy occurs when a person believes that they lack some quality, achievement or possession that another person has. An ugly quality, Aristotle defined envy as 'the pain caused by the good fortune of others'. As one of the church's seven deadly sins, envy is still a powerful force and a disliked quality. That said, envy is behind many advertising campaigns. Few might be willing to admit that they are envious of others yet the subtle power of envy seems to be suggested even in the naming of a well-known perfume with the simple word 'Envy'.

Some of the component parts of envy include those of comparison – what do they have that I don't have; a threatened self-image – I am a lesser person because I don't have what they have and desire – I want what they have. Bertrand Russell was right in suggesting that envy is one of the major causes of unhappiness.

So, how do we get to a place beyond envy? How do we move away from selfishness and develop an attitude of spontaneous kindness? Two issues are vitally important here. First, selfishness – a centring on self – produces a distance from others, a lack of connection to others. In the German novel, *Steppenwolf*, Herman Hesse attempts to produce a modern parable of our times. He paints a picture of an individual who experiences life in two modes of being: his higher or spiritual plane when he is able to connect with others, and his lower or animal being when he lives like a lonely wolf on the steppes of Russia. In this latter mode he is deeply alienated from others – he is truly alone. That aloneness (or disconnection) becomes loneliness and then ultimately becomes a boredom which looks towards thrill-seeking to relieve it. Acts of kindness not only produce connectedness with others; they also flow from a growing awareness that our lives make sense in relationship with others.

Second, engaging in acts of kindness requires a conscious

decision on our part, an act of the will. In just the same way that an athlete must consistently exercise discipline in developing their natural physical abilities, so in the area of kindness we need to consciously decide to engage in acts of kindness. There is an ancient tradition which realized that engaging in acts of kindness can in its own way produce a feeling of boredom along the way. The mystics of old called this state of moral apathy *acedia*. In their view, *acedia* has to be fought with a deliberate decision to overcome apathy, to decide to act kindly as a form of discipline which brings us over time to a reconnection with others, to community and ultimately to happiness.

If we are to make that kind of deliberate choice in favour of kindness, we need some suggestions from which we can design our own programme of fitness in the field of positive action. The following ideas give us a recipe from which to create our own particular dish.

Steps to take

In many senses the list of ways that we can be kind to someone is endless. Whether to friends or complete strangers, whether pre-planned or spontaneous, whether through the giving of our time, or money, or labour, or words there is a lot that we can do to cheer on the life of others.

The top ten we suggest are:

• **Smile** – it is appreciated that you have to be careful with regard to whom you smile at and when you smile and how big your smile is, but smile.

• **Words** – speak kind words, complimentary, true words to people. Be someone who, while still full of integrity, is known for their ability to encourage

51

others. Even more radical, try going for a whole day when you either speak positive things to others or remain silent.

• **Listen** – learn to listen to those who need an ear. It can be hard work and is a deeply neglected and rare quality, but become someone who gives worth to others.

• **Help** – there are so many people today who need a helping hand; perhaps the senior citizen across the road who needs her grass cut or the work colleague who could do with a helping hand.

• **Time** – perhaps the most precious commodity that we have in our action-packed, fast-paced world. What about spending the occasional hour with an elderly neighbour or sitting with your children or grandchildren and talking to them?

• **Money** – so many charities need our hard-earned money. So many noble causes, so many disaster appeals and yet every bit makes a difference. Some of our friends support children growing up in orphanages in the third world. The delight of receiving their letters or of hearing their stories through the sponsoring agencies is heart-warming.

• **Wisdom** – there are many youth organizations or volunteer groups that are crying out for people to come along and share their wisdom with those in desperate need of advice. The joy of giving away what you know and seeing it enlighten another is breath-taking.

• **Surprise** – for many people life is mundane. They feel that they have been on the same boring treadmill for decades. An unexpected bunch of flowers bought for a friend or a selection of delicious cakes from the local bakery for your colleagues or the invite to the local pub with no good reason other than it is a treat will lift everyone's hearts. And yours!

• **Prefer** – if you are in a queue and someone looking hassled joins the queue behind you consider letting them go in front. When shopping, when two of you go for the last packet of hamburgers let the other person have it.

• **Celebrate** – what about identifying those in your community who serve it and then honouring them in some way? Think creatively about how you and your neighbours and friends can honour the people who work in your area as dustmen or postmen, as police or teachers.

Conclusion

On the UK's BBC Radio One station, the presenter Scott Mills has a popular feature on his show called 'Random Acts of Kindness'. As the title suggests, the idea behind the segment is that Mills looks for ways in which he can display a random act of kindness for someone. All of us know someone who could use a little kindness in their lives, but why leave it just to Scott Mills to have all the fun of carrying out random acts of kindness in the lives of others? Every one of us can make a difference to someone else, and as a by-product also make ourselves happier.

Chapter 3

Savour life's joys

Introduction

A lady called Sharon recently returned from a charity trip to Ghana. In describing it, it was obvious she had had an experience of a life time. Preparation for the trip had begun eight months earlier when Sharon had received a phone call from her brother, Lloyd. He leads a charity called Farm4Life, which partners with various projects in Ghana. He wanted to know if she would like to be part of the team going out to this beautiful West African country.

Although Sharon was initially anxious, as the departure date got closer there was a clear build up of anticipation. She checked websites that carried pictures and information about the country, read a number of travel books and had the occasional conversation with friends of friends who had visited the country. By the time she flew out from the airport Sharon was well and truly excited about the wonderful adventure that she had been presented with.

On her return from her African adventure, it was obvious to Sharon's friends that she had lived every moment. Her friends listened to her talking about the 240 photos that covered almost all of the incidents of her trip: she talked about her first-hand experience of the enormous social inequality that is so devastating for those on the wrong side of it; the open sewers, the inadequate health care, the orphanages! Then there was the opportunity to work with Ghanaian nationals who were restoring hope to so many: the cane rat farm, the new businesses that were being stimulated, the schools being modernized and resourced. And she told them about the comical, terrifying and personally heart-wrenching moments that occur on many trips such as these: when one of the team was asked if he was a man or a woman; the mini-bus that had no brakes and, on occasion, failed headlights; the shoe-less three-year-old orphan boy who decided to take her hand and walk with her all day and then fell asleep as he sat on her lap. Five months later and glancing through the photos, Sharon is still reaping the joy of that African safari.

The ability to savour, with its component parts of anticipation for what is about to happen, attention to the moment, appreciation of what is going on and the ability to reminisce, psychologists tell us has the potential to greatly increase our level of happiness. How can we derive greater pleasure from our friendships, activities or unexpected experiences? We need to learn how to savour the good things that are placed on the plate of life!

The skill of savouring enables us to transform any of life's positive experiences into happiness boosters. The good news is that such emotional intelligence can be applied to any of the positive experiences of life. You can be taking a walk with a friend, meeting someone for lunch or glancing through an old photo album – with the right savouring strategy each of these can enhance your quality of life.

How long have you lived?

Anthony Campolo, an American sociologist, presented his class of students with the question, 'How long have you lived?' Initially missing the point of his question one or two spoke out how old they were. 'Twenty-four years,' shouted one student. 'Twenty-three,' called another.

'No,' said the professor. 'I didn't ask how long you had been a breathing, functioning member of the human race. I want you to tell me how long you have been really alive.' Still the students looked confused.

'I want to know,' asked Campolo, 'how long have you lived in the experience of being awe-struck or full of wonder? On how many occasions have you known a heightened awareness of an event that almost took you outside of yourself and caused you to be overwhelmed in and by that moment? How long have you lived?'

In finally understanding what their teacher was alluding to, many of the students acknowledged that they had only been truly alive for a few moments. Savouring opens the door to many more occasions when we are truly alive. It enables us to know what it means to be stilled by the emotion of awe, something that frequently comes with this quality. People who indulge in savouring are often wide eyed, open mouthed, have goose bumps, are brought to tears and find a lump in their throat. When we exercise this emotional muscle we are uplifted.

The ability to savour interacts with the character stength that Seligman calls 'the appreciation of beauty and experience'. This is the capacity to find, recognize and take pleasure in the existence of goodness in the physical and social worlds. To do so in the spiritual world a little more is needed.

The experience of 'transcendence' enables us to forge connections with the larger universe and can provide us with personal meaning. It is grouped with the qualities of gratitude (chapter 1), hope, humour and spirituality.

A simple test to discover whether you have this quality or not, is to remember what it is to have the hairs on the back of your neck stand up or to be moved beyond words. People with this quality are recognized as those who are the life and soul of the party or individuals to whom you would turn if you had something to celebrate.

When it comes to those who possess the ability to savour, Fred Bryant, Professor of Social Psychology at Layola University in Chicago, suggests that although savouring comes easiest to optimists, extroverts and women, this quality is something that can be learned by most people. Those who pursue this skill know that a key to greater happiness is squeezing as much happiness as possible from a happy event and savouring helps you to do this.

The A to Z of savouring!

What is savouring?

On a recent trip to the theatre to watch *Joseph and His Technicolor Dreamcoat*, an elderly woman sat on the front row of the balcony. She was completely caught up in the production. So enthralled was she that during the encore she got up on her feet and started singing and moving along with the music.

This gives an indication of the nature of savouring. To savour is to take the time to appreciate a positive experience. It is about understanding its worth as fully as possible and to enjoy and relish it. Coming from the Latin *sapere*, which means 'to taste', savouring is a psychological term used to describe the concept of being in the moment, being present, being mindful and truly enjoying the experience. It means slowing down, lingering and rejoicing.

Savouring could be defined as any thought or behaviour that enables us to generate, intensify or prolong enjoyment. It is that internal quality which means that, as Ralph Waldo Emerson expressed, 'although we travel the world over to find the beautiful, we must carry it with us or we find it not'.

What does savouring do?

Like a good glass of chilled white wine on a warm summer's evening, savouring enhances life's pleasant experiences. And like a second glass of wine it enlarges positive emotions, thus intensifying and prolonging positive experiences. It can bring to light and help us explore positive events. For some it enables them to recapture the joy of good memories that have faded into the background of their emotional lives. Savouring stops us from only taking the bad from the past, rushing through the present and falsely imagining the future.

How does savouring work?

How savouring an experience actually makes us happier is a conundrum that psychologists have been grappling with for some time. We know that in savouring an experience we are able to convert positive experiences into positive emotions, but how that happens is a little less clear. It's like that ad-hoc dish that you threw together on a Monday night after a busy day at the office. It tasted absolutely delicious, but you can't quite put your finger on what was different about it that made it so.

It has been possible to identify the component parts of the savouring process as our ability to give attention to something and our capacity to appreciate it but it is not clear what triggers the transition from one to the other. Writing in their book *Savouring – A New Model of Positive Experience*, Fred Bryant and Joseph Veroff offer the suggestion that savouring may be seen as a process 'through which people actively derive pleasure and fulfilment in relation to positive experience'. That leaves open the question as to what it is that draws out our appreciation of something!

Why do we need to savour?

The reason we need to savour a positive experience is to reap from it every bit of the happiness it contains. As many of us know, happiness does not consist in things themselves but rather in the relishing that we have of them. What is more, we don't automatically translate positive emotions from good experiences. We need to savour so that we can translate our good experiences into happier lives.

You can be very good at handling every problem that life throws at you but that does not mean that you have the skill to find joy in positive experiences. Being able to manage the sad times does not automatically mean that you will be happy when life is good. It is therefore necessary to learn to savour.

What makes these items sources of pleasure?

Why a blue sky should produce in us a happier disposition than a grey one is a mystery. Why we are drawn to courage and not to cowardice or why more often than not we warm to humility rather than arrogance is not known. Maybe we have an intrinsic pleasure code. In the older western tradition it is said of God that after he had made the world he looked at it and saw that it was good. Perhaps we have something of that awareness of good in us, too. No one needs to tell us that a romantic gesture on the Eiffel Tower is special, and no one needs to tell us that a sunny day is a treat.

Ben Dean, a colleague of Martin Seligman, identifies three types of goodness that we may concentrate on. The first is that of areas of physical or auditory beauty such as a spectacular waterfall. Second, a skill such as the making of a three-tier wedding cake. Third, the abstract areas of virtue or moral goodness such as refusing to scheme or exercise cunning.

What can be savoured?

Almost anything can be savoured, as long as someone is willing to stop and consider through savouring the pleasures these gratifications give. It is possible to savour other people, a seaside town, a walk along the pier, or spending a couple of hours in the sunshine.

One of the charming and humorous eccentricities of Agatha Christie's Belgian detective Hercule Poirot is his delight in Belgian chocolate. How often does he treat himself to a small box for a special occasion and then intentionally eats them one at a time over intervals of several hours? The anticipation, the delight, the lingering taste!

Are there any other advantages of savouring as well as being happier?

Nobel prize winner Daniel Kahneman says that we make our future plans out of our past experiences. If that is so then the capacity to savour ensures that we bring into our present considerations the good outcomes of past decisions. It reminds us of what worked well before.

In addition to the help savouring gives to decision making, various psychologists have mooted ideas of people becoming more optimistic and less depressed; a bolstering of the immune system; speedier recovery from short-term illnesses and a lessening of the risk of illness. It seems that savouring offers us a smorgasbord of delicious benefits.

Can we keep our savouring in check?

Savouring is about enjoying the moment; it is about cherishing events to be re-visited at some future time. However, we do need to avoid trying to capture the moment to the extent that we get engrossed in recording events rather than actually living them. We have probably all witnessed those who want to record the moment with their video camera permanently recording. We understand that they want to capture the scenery, the experience, the sights and sounds of their holiday but what they lose is actually living in the moment. There is a danger that trying too hard to savour the event while it is actually taking place could cause you to lose what the moment is all about. Perhaps the wisest thing we can do in such situations is appreciate that savouring is something that comes after the moment and not in it.

Thank God for Nigella! (How do we savour life's joys?)

When it comes to savouring life's joys, people like Fred Bryant and Martin Seligman have done for us what British cook Nigella Lawson has done for those who struggle in the kitchen. They have given us hope by removing some of the mystery of how to savour and presented us with easily accessible recipes. How do you savour life's joys? You simply take some of the following ingredients and employ them at different times in different situations to ensure that you extract all of the joy that is there.

For some people the annual family holiday can be a bit of a disaster. For many reasons, the vacation does not produce all of the benefits that they had hoped for when booking it. Taking the advice of Bryant and Seligman, there are several things that we can do to ensure that we get the best out of this adventure.

Before we go

Preparing to go gives us an opportunity to look forward to the event. Having placed the dates on our wall planner or in our diary or PDA, we are regularly made aware of this impending adventure. Similar to using an advent calendar, some people may find it worthwhile counting down to when their special event is going to take place.

If we are going on holiday with others then we should ensure that if we ever get together before the holiday we talk about the holiday. We can chat about all that we want to do and our excitement at the upcoming trip.

As the time approaches to leave we can take time to gather information about the area where we will be visiting. It is an opportunity to look at local maps, identify possible places to visit and appreciate some of what is on offer in the area. Like those who thoroughly research the venue for their next city break or next concert or visit to the museum, all information obtained will add to the appreciation of the visit.

When we are there

When we arrive at our destination some of the challenges we face of getting the most out of the experience include trying to *slow down, take time, focus on the now* and then appreciating what we have. There is a movement in Europe named 'Slow Food', which encourages people to take longer to eat and drink old-fashioned, home-cooked food. They feel it is important to give ourselves enough time to taste our food, to spend time with family and friends without rushing. Aware that people rush, rush, rush, these individuals are encouraging people to slow down and take stock. As we gather for our holiday, slowing down will often be our greatest challenge. With everyone having either demanding jobs or busy lives, taking their foot off the accelerator of work will not be easy.

In an attempt to aid people trying to accomplish the goal of decreasing their speed the following suggestions have been made: have a cup of tea; put your feet up; stare out of the window; spend quality time in the bathtub; try and do only one thing at a time; attempt to bring some of your holiday activities into your week.

Next will come the challenge of living in the moment. One of the problems that many of us have is an inability to allow ourselves to enjoy the now. As those who are forever living in the future or in the past, we continually miss the adventure that is happening around us.

In an attempt to help us live and appreciate the now, Dr David Thomas has suggested some simple exercises:

- Take a moment to sit in a comfortable place and observe where you are.

- Ask yourself what is it that you see and then describe the images around you.

- Consider what sounds there are around you; can you smell different smells and if so which are pleasant and which not.

- Tell yourself how the surfaces around you feel

- Attempt to identify the tastes that are in your mouth.

After we return

On returning we can continue to draw joy from our break by facilitating acts of remembrance that reconnect us with it. We could plan a short reunion around a meal. When we get together or if we talk on the phone we can reminisce through storytelling. There are sure to be photos that we can look at or home videos to watch. As we drink the wine that we bought on vacation, there will be recollections of when and where we bought it and moments of shared joy as we recall the sights, sounds and tastes of our time away.

More of Nigella!

In addition to those identified above, other things you can do to savour the moment include:

Simplify

Time is a limited resource and there are many competing demands on it. Is it time for you to review your commitments and your diary, to cut back on some things that you do which crowd out the time you need to savour life?

Deal with issues

Those who are trying to run away from issues in their lives find it very difficult to savour. Perhaps with the help of a friend painful situations need to be faced.

Say thank you

As we express our gratitude so we reinforce the pleasure of the experience.

Seize the moment

A very creative retreat being offered in the UK gives attendees the opportunity to go away for a few days and face their mortality. In a culture that tries to deny the reality of death this insightful group realize that one of the components which sharpens our appreciation of an event is the reality that life is short, fleeting and momentary.

Engage your senses
What can you see, touch, taste, smell or hear?

Open yourself up to the possibility of joy
For some people life is nothing but a struggle. As we live day after day under a cloud we can think that that is the way life has to be. A key moment in the extracting of pleasure from our more positive experiences is giving our self permission to be happy.

A master class on savouring – how can we enhance our savouring skills?

Some training organizations run regular master classes for those learners who are already knowledgeable but want to become experts in their chosen field. When it comes to savouring, the same principle is true, even when we have mastered all of the 'recipes' for savouring there are still developments that can be made to further mature this skill. As we all know, the greater your skill at savouring, the greater your joy in response to positive events. So, in addition to all that we have already mentioned, you can consider taking your savouring to new levels using the following techniques.

Congratulate yourself
Many people have problems accepting a compliment and even fewer engage in any self-talk (speaking to themselves) where they applaud themselves for a job well done.

Assuming that we do not go over the top in congratulating ourselves, there is a place for saying 'well done'.

Share the experience with someone

In J. R. R. Tolkien's *The Lord of the Rings* one of the minor narratives which adds enormous appeal to the book is the fact that the adventure of destroying the ring is shared between a larger group of nine and a smaller team of Frodo and Samwise Gamgee. In the friendship of Frodo and Samwise we have two friends who journey together from their small shire to the fires of Mount Doom. It is together that they leave the other seven to trek across the plains of Mordor. It is together that they struggle with the presence of Gollum and his attempts to take back the ring and it is together that they face death when the mountain explodes and they find themselves marooned on a small rock in a sea of molten lava. In the same way, it is in the company of friends that we are able to face the storms of life, better seize its adventures and add colour to its mundanity. Similarly, our life experiences are deepened by the company of friends.

Take mental photographs

As you go through an experience try to develop the ability to take snapshots in your mind of those involved, the smells, words, colours and tastes.

Compare the experience

We all know people who tend to see the negative side to everything. Whatever the occasion they have that special knack of being able to find something that they think isn't right. Although at times a useful skill, when it comes to developing our ability to savour it is far better to look to the more positive aspects of the experience than the negative ones. Ask yourself the questions: 'What was unique about this experience? How was it better than any similar type of experience that I have had?' In other words, accentuate the positive.

Plan to do more pleasant things

If engaging in pleasant things is the gateway to positive experiences, then plan to do more enjoyable activities.

Appreciate the eternal relevance of what is going on

In the film *Gladiator*, the main character, Maximus Decimus Meridius – played by Russell Crowe – reminds us that what we do in this life echoes in eternity. There is, for all of us, a connection between the actions and experiences of today and that which will fill our eternal tomorrow. With that being the case, my appreciation of every activity has the potential of being deeper. As you think about the things you savour, ask yourself which of those things are purely transitory – here today and gone tomorrow – and which of them carry the potential to have greater significance.

Shout it from the rooftops

Finding ways to express the good things that have happened has the capacity to reinforce their joy to you.

Be absorbed

The more you are able to enter into the experience, the more material you will have to work with as you savour it.

Remind yourself how quickly time flies

How quickly our children grow up. As we get older the seasons seem to come round faster and faster. Therefore, developing the ability to savour gives us an option to slow down and appreciate the moment.

Work at achieving mental quiet

Our minds can be filled with so many voices, so many thoughts all vying for our attention. Despite the effort required a very worthwhile activity is that of working on how we quieten our minds – it is all to do with exercising control and disciplining our thoughts.

Freeing our palette (What stops us from savouring?)

There are a number of obstacles that get in the way of us savouring the moment. Some are obvious and others less so. As we begin to identify and then remove these taste blockers we will be able to fully live the experience.

Over-connectedness

We can be robbed of the joy of talking with a friend because we are bombarded by a variety of contacts instantly. As we sit at our computer talking with a friend on Skype we can also be on MSN, emailing someone, reading a text and waiting for a phone call.

Over stimulation

If you have ever been to a Disney park you will have experienced the songs that go on playing in your head even after you have left the park. The sights, the sounds, the thrilling rides all add up to a great day out but they also illustrate the variety of stimuli that we encounter every day. All of this can make savouring an initially cold and boring activity as some of what we savour is less multi-sensory and more simplistic – a homemade birthday card or an email from an old friend whom we haven't seen for a while, for instance. This reminds us that it is good to take pleasure in simple things, too.

Culture

The consumer myth is that happiness is found in purchasing what you do not have. The spirit of savouring is enjoying what you already have rather than going in search of what you do not have.

The wrong value system

Is there anything as wonderful as an hour sitting and talking with your small child? Is there anything as enjoyable as going for a walk with your teenage son and talking about future hopes and possibilities? Is there anything more delightful than spending an evening in the company of the person you love? Is there anything as stimulating as meeting friends for lunch or chatting for hours over several cups of delicious coffee? We have to be so careful that some of the meaningless values of media advertising do not re-write our own more worthwhile value system.

Thinking like a kill-joy

On so many occasions a moment of joy is lost because of negative thoughts that fill our minds. What will others think of what we are doing? I wish I had something else rather than this! I wish I was at that place rather than this one! To fully enter the moment it is so important that we learn to manage these thoughts. As part of this, one of the skills that we have to grow is the one that enables us not to fix our thoughts on one negative comment that is made in the middle of hundreds of positive ones.

Setting the timer

Although time for some means money, in all probability time is more valuable than money. If we lose all our money we usually still have the capacity to earn more. Not so with time. Savouring needs time. It is not something that can be rushed or engaged in with a variety of other things. It is because of that that effort needs to be made to stay in control of how we spend our time.

We need to manage our time, to learn to say 'no', to make time for things, to ensure that we are not too busy to give enough time to things, to be aware of the weakness of spreading ourselves too thinly, to ensure that we are not weighed down by having too much on our plate, to avoid so living in the urgent that we are rushing from one experience to the other. It is important that we watch that our focus is not easily taken by something else.

One of the most important questions that we need to ask ourselves when it comes to nurturing our savouring capabilities relates to the compromises we are making on our happiness because of time pressures.

Savouring God

The sacred text that belongs to the older western tradition encourages us to 'taste and see that the Lord is good'. We need to take time to explore and savour the spiritual dimension of life.

Steps to take

From all that we have said about savouring it is easy to see why this is one of the steps towards a happier life. But where do you actually begin? How do you go about dabbling in this life-transforming ability? Here are some suggestions to get you started.

- Plan a perfect day. Take some time over several
  nights to plan what for you would be the perfect

day and then look through your diary so you can set a time when you will enjoy that perfect day. If possible, take someone along with you to enjoy your day. If you can't do a perfect day do a half day.

- Go to a museum and pick out a piece of artwork or a display that has aesthetic value and touches you because of its beauty.

- Write down your thoughts about a piece of art or something beautiful you see as you travel to work.

- Use a camera to hone in on something beautiful.

- Take a walk with a friend and comment on something beautiful you see.

- Attend a concert and listen to one appreciatively on headphones at night. Or ask a friend to recommend the most beautiful music he or she knows.

- Plan a daily and, if possible, weekly mini-vacation. Schedule into your life what you may do on holiday; read through a book or the daily paper; people-watch.

- Keep a journal and record something you saw during the day that struck you as extremely beautiful or skilful.

Chapter 4

Thank a mentor

Introduction

Steve Thomas recently went to say goodbye to his friend and mentor, Mike Atkins. For over twenty years Mike had been actively involved in Steve's life but over a couple of weeks it had become obvious that he was losing his heroic fight against cancer. One month after visiting his dear friend, Mike passed away.

Their friendship had begun when Steve was appointed as one of the leaders of the voluntary organization that Mike led. With an instant connection, they very quickly became good friends and Mike gradually took the role of father figure. He helped Steve better understand the dynamics of the organization, showing him how to lead volunteers, how to instil vision and to keep going even when no positive outcome could be seen. When Steve moved on to take up full-time leadership of a different group, Mike continued to be a trusted advisor, helping him grapple with understanding the big picture and working through the smaller details of an organization's life.

In talking with Steve about that day, it was obvious that for both him and Mike it was a very emotional one. Knowing the prognosis, he spontaneously took the opportunity to thank Mike for his friendship, his care and all that he had invested into his life. There was a fair bit of joking as they reminisced about the early days of their relationship and also moments of gratitude as they remembered how very difficult situations had worked out so well. It is a day that still brings deep, deep joy to Steve.

Everyone has a mentor, whether knowingly or not. We are all influenced by someone or possibly a number of people throughout our lives.

Martin Seligman and others suggest that joy is experienced through the ritual of taking time to thank these mentors. Chris Peterson, a psychology professor at the University of Michigan, says that we will see measurable improvements in our mood through engaging in such visits. Studies have shown that for a full month after a gratitude visit happiness levels tend to go up, while boredom and other negative feelings go down. For most people, the gratitude visit is the most effective exercise for raising levels of happiness. With that in mind we are going to look in this chapter at how to thank a mentor.

Looking good naked

When it comes to defining what we mean by 'mentor' it is fair to say that there is a broad range of definitions. At the most basic level, a distinction is made between those who are interested in the person and those who focus on the task. A coach asks you 'How is the task going?' while a mentor asks 'How are you doing?'

The word 'mentor' can be used to refer to someone who has particular mentoring skills and/or for someone whom we admire, has influence in our lives and is some type of hero.

73

For the purposes of this chapter a mentor is defined as someone who has influenced your life for good – either now or in the past. They are those who have contributed to making you a better person, be that physically, emotionally, financially, gastronomically, psychologically, spiritually, academically, fashionably, career-wise, sociably or relationally. They are those whom you would consider to be your trusted advisors, counsellors or teachers.

It doesn't matter whether this relationship is formal or informal, these are the voices that you listen to. It could be your team leader at work or your grandmother. As far as the history of the concept is concerned, we first read about 'Mentor' in Homer's *Odyssey*. Mentor was the son of Alcumus, who in later life became the friend of Odysseus. Odysseus later asked him to take charge of his son when he left to take part in the Trojan War. Although not the noblest of characters, Mentor is identified as the archetype of this role. The modern usage of the term is to be found in a book by François Fénelon entitled *The Adventures of Telemachus*.

This is the origin of our contemporary idea of a mentor being someone who is a wise friend or guide. Foundational to many of the emerging mentoring programmes, it carries the idea of a more experienced person nurturing a novice. Perhaps one of the most significant but unsung mentors about today, who is having a very positive impact on so many vulnerable people, is Gok Wan. Presenter of the British television programme *How to Look Good Naked*, Gok is someone who takes as much time to nurture the inner beauty and self-worth of a person as he does developing their dress sense.

Everybody's at it

A surprising side to mentoring is that so many people are doing it, whether that be through work or sport or voluntary organizations set up to nurture young people. Mentoring cuts across a common idea of a person's independence. As we noted above we would argue that we are all following someone, though more often than not this is done subconsciously.

Everyone has been trained by someone else at some point in life, but many of the most successful people in the world have had special mentoring relationships! Socrates mentored Plato. In turn Plato advised Aristotle. Aristotle went on to counsel Alexander the Great. More recently, Oprah Winfrey has spoken about the influence of her fourth grade teacher who helped her believe in herself. General Colin Powell cites the great example of his father. Added to these could be Richard Branson, who was mentored by Freddie Laker; Lance Armstrong, who was mentored by fellow Tour de France winner Eddy Merckx and Rosa Parks, who was mentored by her teacher Alice White.

If a rationale for mentoring was needed then one could be found in some of the consequences that come out of forming such a relationship: the opportunity to not make the same mistakes as others, to grow into a better person, to tap into the wisdom of others and the possibility of being introduced to different networks. For the mentor there is the chance of investing in the life of others and of making a lasting difference.

Applauding your mentor

There are numerous ways that you can express thanks to your mentor. Perhaps one of the most unique ways of expressing gratitude was that shown by Samuel Eto'o, a soccer player from Cameroon. He reputedly changed his surname to that of the man who helped him realize his dream of becoming a professional soccer player. For those who will find the notion of making a gratitude visit, with its component parts of going to someone who has powerfully influenced their life and reading them a letter, just a little bit too much then some of the following may work.

Thank you treat

In getting to know your mentor you will have picked up some of the ways that they like to treat themselves. Taking the time to arrange one of these is a lovely way of saying thank you. How much enjoyment there is in booking someone a pampering day or buying them a really nice bottle of wine.

Thank you celebration

Teacher Appreciation Day is an opportunity for students to say thank you to the person who has shaped them over the last academic year. What about holding one of those for the club coach or your company's Human Resources Officer? If several of you have the same life coach, perhaps take them out and spoil them. Why just say thank you on your own? Try and get as many people involved as possible. It multiplies the enjoyment!

Thank you video

A novel idea might be to make your own thank you video, then show it to your mentor and then put it on the Internet site YouTube for everyone else to enjoy!

Eulogies are strange things. Most people use them as an opportunity to say all the things that they really admired about someone. They talk about their accomplishments and particularly about the influence that the deceased person had on their lives. Like obituaries, it is just a pity that these words were not spoken to the person when they were alive. It would have been a lot more fun!

The gratitude visit

In the spirit of the eighteenth-century 'visit of thanks' we want to look at the practicalities of making a gratitude visit. The idea is simple: you choose someone who has positively influenced your life and then after writing them a letter which expresses your gratitude you meet up with them and read the letter to them.

Very few people will have ever made a gratitude visit or written a letter for such an occasion, so outlined below is a suggested step-by-step process for undertaking such a visit or letter.

Choose an important person from your past who has influenced your life

Identify someone who has invested in your life whom you have never taken the opportunity to appropriately thank. Obvious candidates can include a teacher from school or a lecturer from university or your first boss or a dear friend or close relative. It may even be a parent! Pick out someone who has positively shaped your life for the good.

Write them a testimonial letter

This is not one of the easiest tasks to do and will almost certainly seem inadequate for the occasion but nevertheless do attempt to pen a letter of thanks. We will look at what to include in the letter later on in the chapter.

Meet up with them

There is no hard and fast rule as to where you should meet. What do you think would be best for them? If it is appropriate you could meet them in their home or if it is better for them, at their office. If they would feel comfortable you could invite them to your own home. What is important is that when it comes to reading the letter you have composed to them they are not going to be distracted by too much noise or activity going on around them.

Don't tell them in advance what you're going to do

This is a difficult one to manage, but it adds to the surprise and therefore the joy that both of you experience.

Laminate the testimonial as a gift

Either laminate or frame your letter. It adds to the occasion and gives them the opportunity of reading your grateful words again and again.

Read them the letter

It would be a good idea to practise reading the letter through several times before you visit. Like practising your kissing in the mirror, however artificial it is you begin to get an idea of what the experience is going to be like.

When it comes to reading your letter live, take your time, read with expression and try and maintain eye contact as much as possible.

Let the other person react unhurriedly

This may be a first for both you and your mentor. Give them time to savour the experience. Do not force a response, don't look for some quick comforting applauding words back. Relax and allow them to speak at their own pace and respond in their own way.

Reminisce together

Although the sun is not going to come out and the birds are not going to start singing and a rainbow is not going to appear in the sky it will feel like it. So, as the memories and stories begin to be told sit back and enjoy a cocktail of joyful shared experiences.

Be prepared for masses of emotion

They may smile, they may cry, they may get up and hug you, they may start laughing. Who knows for sure how they will respond? But respond they will.

Composing a letter of thanks

Attempt to write the letter so that it fills one sheet of paper. It needs to be long enough to say what you want to say but not too long so that when you are reading it the emotion becomes too great or what you are reading seems too thin.

It is important to take your time writing this letter. Don't think about rushing to compose it. Even when every word feels like giving birth to your first child keep going. You will be pleasantly surprised at what you have managed to put together when the letter is done.

Don't worry about getting the letter right on your first attempt; quite often people will create several drafts before they begin to have confidence in what they have written.

The content of the letter should be as detailed as possible. A general thanks for being your mentor is nice, but one that picks up on particular contributions that you feel the mentor has made to your life is far more meaningful for both of you.

The key to composing any letter of gratitude is to take a good amount of time to reflect on your relationship with your mentor. With a reservoir of stories to draw from or points to make the letter will take shape with substance and flair.

Try and write the best letter that you can. Be yourself and do your best and don't worry about it not being good enough. The person that you are going to read this to knows you fairly well. They know what you are like, where you have been and where you are going and they can tell what is genuinely yours and what is not. They can also recognise the amount of effort you have put into it.

As far as the content of the letter is concerned, you could include some or all of the following: something that you have not said before; your first impressions; what you have learned; a special memory; your intention to mentor others and/or pass on what you have learned; thoughts about the next phase of your relationship.

Passing on the baton

In addition to making a gratitude visit one of the most satisfying ways of saying thank you to your mentor is to pass what you have learned on to others. Unless you were born knowing everything you know now, there have been people throughout your life who have taken the time to invest something of themselves in you. One of the greatest compliments that you can give to your mentor is to pass that on to others.

Many people feel that they are not special enough to be a mentor to anyone, but whether we like it or not, there are probably lots of people looking at us and following our example. There are individuals whom we are totally unaware of hanging on our every word. You don't need to be a prizewinner to set an example for others to follow – just be yourself and allow the good things that are in you to hang out wherever you go.

One is never too old or too young to be mentored and one is never too old or too young to mentor others. There are countless numbers of young people and some older who need an example to follow. Scott Peck cites how, through the breakdown of society, many people lack basic life skills.

The absence of these fundamental character tools threatens to create tragically ruined lives. For us, the challenge in all of this is having something worth passing on.

Choosing your mentor wisely – looking for a hero

From glancing at the latest film releases it is obvious that people are still looking for heroes and heroines to follow. Often these are viewed almost as demigods who display either incredible powers or a quality of character that causes them to find courage in the most overwhelming of situations or the ability to sacrifice themselves for the good of others.

Our idea of what makes a hero changes over time. Whereas our heroes in the twentieth century might have been Martin Luther King Jr, Robert F. Kennedy, Nelson Mandela, Rosa Parks or Mohandas K. Gandhi, today, for some, heroes are celebrities who are famous – for being famous.

Accepting our earlier premise that everyone has someone they admire, it would be interesting to stop and consider who it is that we look to and why that may be. What is it exactly that we find so attractive that causes us to be influenced by their example?

In reflecting on this, we suggest the following list of qualities to look for in a mentor. It is by no means an exhaustive list, but it is a starting point to set us thinking.

An example worth following

In many senses it goes without saying, but you want to be following someone who is worth learning from – someone who has the expertise or role or gives an example of what you would want to have for yourself. As we noted above, there are some serious questions to be asked about what makes this person worth following. It is pretty pitiful if the only reason that you choose to follow someone is because they have money or fame or a nice car or house or an attractive partner.

Accessible

How frustrating it would be to have as your mentor someone with incredible knowledge and expertise but who is too busy to meet with you. Or, when they can see you it is for five minutes in between classes or projects. Accessibility says something about their commitment to you. There comes a point in your training when you need to be able to sit down and chat through the issues that you are working on. Rather than five minutes of pontificating from your mentor you need someone who is going to share the journey with you.

Commitment to you

You want to follow someone who believes in you, who is not going to give up on you when you fail again, who is willing to invest in you with an openness to see what happens. Through work mentoring programmes there are agreed procedures, but even there you want to look out for the mentor who is interested in you for who you are and not just for what skills you can be taught to contribute to the good of the company.

Teachable

Why some people act as if they know it all is a mystery to us. Teachability is an incredibly admirable trait and if a mentor has this they are less likely to get stuck because of their own limited personal resources. We all want to follow someone who is going somewhere and who is likely to get there; someone who is cutting the mustard today and will probably cut it tomorrow, not someone who cut the mustard twenty-five years ago and that was it. A willingness to learn gives such a person hope.

Someone of character

Companies today want to be led by people of character. Of course they need to know what they are doing but they also have to have attractive personalities. Who they are is as important as what they can do. The thinking is that who they are shapes how they will work out what they know. When it comes to setting company culture, the character of those in leadership has an enormous impact.

We believe that everyone is created uniquely, in so becoming someone's protégé it is wise to find someone who will work with the image that has been placed within you and makes you you.

An attractive spiritual mentor

As for finding a spiritual mentor, it is very important that time be taken to consider the qualities of the person you want to be taught by.

If we take the Christian model of Jesus as our example, then we are looking for a spiritual guide who shares some of his merits. We should want to follow someone who has an attractive character, speaks wise words, expresses a deep interest in those around them and has some awareness of the God of the older western tradition.

Conclusion

In reflecting on the significant relationship that Steve and Mike shared, one of the factors that was foundational to its beginning and longevity was the humility and openness to learning of both men. Neither of them pretended that they knew it all. Initially the teaching was going one way, but over time a balance was struck as both opened their thinking up to the other. Recognizing our own limitations is often one of the best ways to rid ourselves of them.

Chapter 5

Learn to forgive

Introduction

How good are you at getting revenge? The saying goes that 'revenge is a dish best served cold'. If that's true for you, what are your top five ways of getting even? If somebody makes cruel comments behind your back at work or one of your best friends decides to break a confidence and tell everyone your secret, how do you get your own back?

A friend of ours told us how when she was a teenager one of the ways that she made one of her boyfriends pay for splitting up with her was to graffiti obscene remarks about him on his car. This backfired and she received an official letter of complaint. Some people find that a juicy rumour works well. It doesn't really matter if it is true or not. In the book and film *Notes on a Scandal*, the life of Cate Blanchett's character, Sheba Hart, is destroyed because of a vicious piece of gossip started by a fellow teacher, Barbara Covett, played in the film by Judi Dench. Admittedly, it was true but the motivation for informing was not for the good of either the teacher or the pupil but rather the desire for inducing pain.

Then there is the silent treatment. This may mean

excluding someone. A big social event is organized at work and you make sure that the one person who is not invited is the person who hurt you. A more subversive approach is to turn their friends against them. It takes some thought and strategic action but a good plan can normally see a group of friends turn against the person who betrayed you. If all else fails then it is only doing to them what they did to you!

If the truth be told, there is an endless list of ways of getting even. Many of the films being released or books currently being published offer ideas to those wanting to get their own back on someone.

The challenge of forgiveness

It is not too difficult to understand the notion of vengeance. Although the illustrations above are slightly trivial, when it comes to the deeper stuff, there is very little debate to be had about whether someone has the right to see their perpetrator suffer.

From the dawn of civilization the concept of vengeance or blood feuds has been part of society. In Japanese culture this is particularly so. One of the roles of the samurai was to uphold family honour, which would include revenge killing. The problem is that any retaliation for a wrongdoing can easily exceed what others may consider a fair response. That's why one of the pillars of the legal system is that of just revenge. Not only is personal retribution injurious rather than harmonious but it also needs to be limited.

In addition to the concept of personal revenge or in its noblest disguise justice, what also works against us offering forgiveness is our own basic make-up. As Seligman points out, we naturally gravitate to the darker side of our character rather than our more generous nature. Stronger than the good that is in us, this mentality would far rather see someone suffer for the wrong that they did us than allow us to pardon them for their crimes.

If you observe the wrong actions of one friend against another, one of the added stumbling blocks to you offering forgiveness is that it apparently disrespects the pain being suffered by the victim. This is a particularly difficult situation to navigate when good friends who are couples end up separating because of an affair. How do you remain close to both of them when one feels that you should completely reject their former partner?

Not a pretty picture

There is another take on the effects of being ill-treated by another that flows from the harm that the actions of others have had on us both in the sense of how easy our hatred or desire for revenge can twist us as human beings and how the pain that we felt can cause us to lose our balance.

We may be tempted to laugh at the intensity of Captain Ahab's hatred for Moby Dick, or the cold-blooded passion with which Edmond Dantes in *The Count of Monte Christo* has worked out his scheme to make those who hurt him suffer, but it isn't too difficult to see the self-damage that not being able to let go of hating someone can have on you.

We may not turn out like Darth Vader, but we all know people who have been so riddled with bitterness that you would swear that they were his double – completely riddled with loathing towards someone. There was a TV chat show recently which focused on the issue of revenge. It's easy to understand why the people hated those who had abused them – some of them had suffered terribly at the hands of others – but there was also no mistaking the crippling effect that such hatred was having on these victims.

Rob Bell, a commentator on spirituality, has an interesting angle on the impact of those who act against us and the consequences of such actions on us. Offering his video commentary at an airport he suggests that we are all carrying wounds – wounds that have negatively shaped us, wounds which cause us to act out of character, and wounds which stop us from living full lives. Like those at the airport, we find ourselves travelling with luggage that is not too easy to get about with.

It's important to remind ourselves that revenge and the pain caused by the wrong actions of others is not something that is experienced only on a personal level. Whether it be the tragedy of the Twin Towers or the continuing Israeli-Palestinian conflict, the presence of a vendetta mentality only fuels a cycle of conflict.

What is forgiveness?

The question of what we understand by forgiveness is a very important one. A woolly or outwardly false definition has the potential to prevent us breaking free and, even worse, possibly lead us into even greater agony.

Forgiveness is breaking free

Many years ago a local postman returned home from work to see a crowd of people gathered at one of the houses in his street. A boy had got his hand stuck in the letter box and was unable to get free. Those who had gathered had tried everything to release the boy and in desperation were about to call the fire brigade. Within a few moments of arriving at the scene the postman had got the boy's hand out of the letter box. How did he do it? He had managed to talk the boy into letting go of what he was holding on to. Forgiveness enables us to let go of the bitterness or revenge or pain that we are holding on to. It makes it possible for us to be free.

Forgiveness is making a shift in our thinking

We are talking about the journey from wanting to ruin the lives of those who hurt us to not being too bothered whether they succeed in life or not. It is the climb from wanting to kill them to being able to sit in the same room as them. It is the marathon of having nothing but bad things to say about them to being able to bite our tongue when we are asked what we think of them. It does not necessarily mean becoming best friends with them, but it does mean not viewing them as 'the enemy'.

Forgiveness is re-writing history

If gratitude helps us to promote the good things that have happened during the course of our lives then unforgiveness has the ability to magnify our negative experiences. With these darker moments come all the emotions that stifle us. Not only that, but they also block contentment and satisfaction. Forgiveness offers us the option of transforming bad memories. It does not take away the memories but it can help remove the sting of them. We get the opportunity to re-write the impact that our past has on us today.

Forgiveness is working at countering certain emotions

In her book, *The How of Happiness,* Sonja Lyubomirsky suggests that forgiveness involves the suppressing or mitigating of one's motivation for avoidance or revenge. It creates a space with which to replace them with more positive attitudes towards the person who injured us.

Forgiveness is not...

Forgetting
Although the Bible may say that God is able to forgive and forget, that is not what it means for us to forgive, nor is it what happens when you do forgive someone for the hardship they caused you. On some occasions it would be wonderful if, when you forgave someone the wrong they did against you, it was erased from your memory, but sadly that cannot happen. You could attempt to suppress these memories but it is probably not going to be good for you.

Pardoning
When someone acts outside of the law there are consequences. On occasions when you are mistreated, your offering of forgiveness does not remove from that person the consequences of or accountability for their actions.

Condoning
No one deserves someone to act wrongly towards them. Any argument put forward that suggests you had it coming to you is simply unpalatable.

Excusing
When someone acted to hurt you they did it for a reason. They were responsible for their actions. OK, they might have been high on drugs, but they decided to take those drugs. There is absolutely no place for trying to explain their actions away as if it wasn't really their fault. That does not help them and it does not help us.

Reconciliation
Forgiveness can on occasion open up the possibility of a future that includes the one who has damaged you but it

is not part of what forgiveness means. The husband who gradually gets to a place where he can forgive his wife for beating him should not be expected to then move back into the family home. The secretary who has been sexually harassed by her boss should not be expected to go back into the office after finding it in her heart to forgive him.

Implying denial of harm

When we forgive someone for something they have done against us, we are in no way undermining the pain that it caused us. In fact, it can be argued that true forgiveness can only be given when we have considered the pain that we have suffered. We may think that premature forgiveness makes it easier for us to cope with the wrongdoing we have suffered, but it helps neither us nor the one who caused us harm. Forgiveness is a wonderful quality, something that can enhance our lives, but it is not wishy-washy. It is tough love and as such faces the reality of the situation and deals with it.

Why forgive?

Forgiveness is a good life strategy; for it has the potential of making us happier people. It has the potential to enable us to re-write our history, help us to break free from the wounds that hurt us so much, counter damaging emotions and assist us to reconfigure our thinking. Each and every one of these presents us with the possibility of becoming happier. There are many other reasons why forgiving someone is good for you.

Forgiveness can change the end of the story

It is said that nearly every story has one of three endings: revenge, tragedy or forgiveness. Forgiveness actually opens the door to another chapter.

It breaks the cycle of avoidance and vengeance

Our natural response to being hurt by someone is to react negatively, to avoid the person and to seek revenge. All of these can make us unhappy and potentially destroy any relationship that existed. Forgiveness can break that cycle.

It improves your health

Links have been made between hostility and heart disease. Those with explosive voices, a pent-up anger and who are outwardly angry are five times more likely to have heart problems. Whereas those who are able to forgive a grudge may well see their blood pressure go down, their resting heart rate decrease and their immune system get stronger. Not only that, but forgiveness has the potential of alleviating irritable bowel syndrome, decreasing headaches, backaches and neck pain and strengthening sexual drive.

It opens up the possibility of restored relationships

Forgiveness does not mean that you have to be reconciled to someone, but it does open up the possibility. When John and Anne argued it was always explosive. Tragically on one occasion the comments were so vicious that John felt that he had to get out of the family home. With both of them being unable to apologize they separated, and after a period of time were divorced They now live lonely, painful lives. The giving of an apology and the offer and receiving of forgiveness could have changed that outcome.

It enables a person to move on

Those who have not offered forgiveness find themselves wandering helplessly in their own personal maze of pain and debilitation. There is no way out, there is no going forward, they are locked in a small area trapped by their hurt. Forgiveness cuts a straight path from wherever they are out of that place.

It frees us from our wounds

Our wounds become sensitive areas in our lives. If someone accidentally nudges against us we overreact and explode at them. We can find ourselves overcompensating for where we are experiencing pain. We close off parts of our lives because we can't take another beating there. Forgiveness has the potential of bringing healing to those parts of our lives which distress us. It will leave scars, but that will be an indication that the open wound has now been cleansed and healed.

It stops us from hurting ourselves

Although we may cause a repentant perpetrator a small degree of discomfort by our unwillingness to forgive them, that is nothing compared to the hurt that we are causing ourselves. As noted above, forgiving someone opens up the possibility of moving on, becoming free and breaking from the negative cycles at work in us. There is a Buddhist quote that says, 'Holding on to anger is like grasping a hot coal with the intent of throwing it at someone else, but you are the one who gets burned.'

It works for the good of society

Beneath the thin veneer that many of us put up, there is pain. Often people feel that they are alone in their suffering. The exercising of forgiveness opens us up to the reality that we are not alone. It also strengthens our personal relationships and our sense of connection with others.

It helps the person who harmed us

An argument put forward by some is that forgiveness is something that we should do for ourselves and not for the person who wronged us. We can understand that argument and in many senses can agree with the sentiment. However, part of being a member of the human race is that we strive for the good of others and not just ourselves. We are all injured in some way and therefore act inappropriately at our weakest times. When that does happen what we need is to have those whom we have hurt forgive us. There is a case for saying, 'What goes around comes around'. You may be familiar with the Lord's Prayer, which says, 'Forgive us our sins as we forgive those who sin against us.' How can we expect people to forgive us if we do not forgive others? Forgiveness is the refusal to hurt the one who hurt you. We are talking about burying the hatchet but not in the perpetrator.

How do you forgive?

So how do we wipe the slate clean? Although it may be more difficult for men to do this than women – according to research men hold on to grudges and hurts longer than women – how do we travel to the place where we have changed our mind about someone and let go of the hurt that we have? At the outset it must be acknowledged that this is not a quick or easy journey.

Part of what follows was taken from the work of psychologist Everett Worthington, who devised a strategy for forgiving people called REACH. Tragically and heroically he worked this out in practice when his aged mother was brutally raped.

Weigh up if you want to forgive this person or not

It's your choice. No one can force you to forgive someone. You are the only one who can make that decision. Part of that decision is weighing up the pros and cons of doing so. As we have already identified, healing from the hurts we feel requires change. But you have to decide if you want to make that change. The older western tradition would add that it is only when we forgive others that we can know forgiveness ourselves, but again that is a choice we must personally make.

If this is a trek that we choose to go on then it would be helpful to formulate a rationale for the journey. Such a rationale could be 'I have decided to forgive David for what he did to me because I can then be free from the hurt he caused.' It is important at this stage to carefully consider your destination. What does forgiveness mean? What does it mean for you?

Personally journey to a place of forgiveness

We can identify four stages to reaching the destination of offering forgiveness.

To begin with there is the recalling of the hurt that you have experienced. This needs to be faced honestly and in as objective a way as possible. This is probably best done in the company of a really good friend.

Next, attention should be given to trying to understand the point of view and reasons why the person who hurt you could have done that to you. This is not about you finding justification for their actions in your own weaknesses – a sort of deserved punishment.

Then, it is time to think about a moment when someone has forgiven you. Try and recall what that was like. Review the distance they must have travelled, the confusion and pain your actions would have caused them. Reminisce about the delight you experienced at their forgiveness.

Lastly, you need to set your mind to forgive. This will include a letting go of your own hurt and also a desire to think about them differently.

Decide on the best way of expressing forgiveness – for you and for them

There are at least three options available to you. You can arrange to go and see them and talk to them about what they did to you and offer them forgiveness. It may be a good idea to take someone along with you.

Alternatively, you could write them a letter detailing what they did and how that has affected you and expressing your forgiveness of them.

In some situations the best way of expressing forgiveness is to reach that point personally but never tell the person concerned. This is a wise way forward if they don't know that they hurt you and that your informing them of the fact would damage them more than by being forced to consider the wrongdoing and receive your forgiveness. This could also be the best way ahead if making contact with them is simply a foolish or dangerous thing to do.

What we are looking to do in all of these is express the words 'I forgive you'.

Walk out your new mindset

What that means is for you to decide. If forgiveness means letting go of your hurt then there will be an element of taking control of it. If forgiveness also means wishing the best for the other person then forgiveness means not talking negatively about them, not looking to destroy them. There may be an element of restoring relationships but that is not a prerequisite of forgiving someone.

Hold on to forgiveness

When Heather forgave Richard for the affair he had had, she thought that would be the end of the angry and painful thoughts she had suffered because of his stupidity. Surprisingly for her, they kept coming. They almost always came unexpectedly and occasionally with intense emotion. What Heather discovered was that she needed to hold on to the attitude that she had journeyed to and to use that to check her emotions. Although not easy, gradually things began to change. She still gets those moments when she feels that she is living the event all over again – especially when she sees the other woman around town – but they are now far less intense and less frequent.

As is obvious from the steps outlined above, this is no easy journey. Like risking the rush to buy concert tickets for your favourite rock band, this is not a trip for the faint-hearted. For those who nevertheless determine to travel towards this destination perhaps the journey is made easier by the companionship of friends or an advisor. What should encourage us is that those who make it to their desired destination find a banquet of positive consequences.

Steps to take: building your forgiveness muscles

We know from our own lives that forgiving someone is not easy. It has been suggested that of all the happiness promoting strategies, forgiveness is the hardest to put into practice. It is even more difficult than having to accept that you are really a dress size larger than you wish to admit, or having to buy jeans for a larger waist than you had imagined. Since that is the case, it is important to regularly spend time developing the muscles that we will need to express forgiveness.

Some of these, as Sonja Lyubomirsky suggests, will include the following.

Appreciating being forgiven

Take some time to remember an occasion when someone forgave you. Imagine what they would have had to work through, the pain you caused them, the choice they wrestled with of forgiving or not and then the way in which they expressed their forgiveness?

Seeking forgiveness

Consider if there is anyone that you have intentionally harmed. If so, what about writing them a letter or thinking through making them a visit and letting them know what you did and asking for their forgiveness.

Imagining forgiveness

Take your time and imagine what it would be like to forgive the person who has wronged you. Ask yourself questions like 'How did they make me feel?' and 'What would it be like to forgive them?' Imagine how you would offer them forgiveness.

Writing a letter of forgiveness

You don't need to send the letter, but what about taking the time to pen a letter that expresses the anger and bitterness you feel? Let the person know what they did to you and then offer them forgiveness.

Reading the stories of others who have forgiven someone

Type Nelson Mandela into Google and read his story. Look at the words he spoke when he was finally released from prison. Search news websites and read the stories of ordinary people who have acted extraordinarily in the way they have offered forgiveness to those who have robbed them of a partner or child through reckless driving or violent knife crime.

Talking to those who have expressed forgiveness
Sit down over lunch with one of your friends whom you know has worked through an issue and forgiven someone. Ask them to talk you through their experience.

Practising empathy
People who can feel for other people are better at expressing forgiveness than those who cannot. Through the day stop and consider the feelings of others.

Focusing less on those occasions when someone has hurt you
It is far too easy to focus on those feelings of bitterness and dwell on those moments of hurt rather than chew on joy experienced with those who have been your friends for a long time. Try and make a conscious effort to not spend time digging up your feelings of hurt. It will intensify your feelings and make it harder for you to offer forgiveness or to stay in the place of having offered forgiveness.

More than one type of forgiveness

Although we have focused on the offering of forgiveness from one person to another, it must be observed that there are other types of forgiveness. Of equal importance to many psychologists is forgiving yourself. The argument is simple you cannot be happy unless you are happy with yourself. The journey towards self-delight is on the road of personal forgiveness. There will be things about yourself that you do not appreciate; you will act in ways that you wish you did not. How do you deal with these? You deal with these by forgiving yourself.

An area picked up by the Dalai Lama in his book *The Art of Happiness* connects with the idea of being someone who is on the end of someone else's forgiveness. Citing how we all suffer from guilt induced by our failure to love someone else as we should or because we have acted towards them in a way that has hurt them, he encourages us to restore that broken relationship.

In considering the landscape of the older western tradition, a missing piece in most of the conversations around forgiveness is that of our need to be reconciled in our relationship with the divine creator who has expressed himself in the person and teaching of Jesus. Considering that there is an incredible interest in the spiritual, it is surprising that this is such a neglected area.

This call to reconnect with our creator is illustrated in the story Jesus told about a father who had two sons. One day the younger son asked for his share of the family estate so that he may head off and enjoy life more fully. The father, appreciating that love must be offered and not forced, allowed his boy to go. The story recounts that for a time the younger son had a great time but then his money ran out and he found himself in a miserable place. Wisely, this boy decided to return home with the hope that his father might at least hire him as a servant. The story ends with the father seeing his son coming home and running to him, dressing him in the finest clothes and threw for him the best of parties. The point that Jesus was making is that all of us have wandered away from God and that what we will discover on reconnecting with him is a very enthusiastic response.

The spiritual dynamic

In exploring the pathway of forgiveness to happiness, it is important to pause for a moment and consider the contribution that the spiritual offers us. After all, there is a spiritual dynamic to forgiveness and not just a psychological one!

Psychologists note that forgiveness is easier for those who are aware of their spiritual capacities, but why is that so? Those who speak of being forgiven by God report that the impact of that encounter brings a strong motivation to forgive others. What is more, this belief system promises a power to embrace the challenge of forgiveness (the energy of God within us) and asks that on occasion we consider forgiving someone more than once.

Added to these are the possibilities that are opened up through prayer. Although few psychologists would want to specify who people pray to, there is agreement that it aids in the search for forgiveness.

Conclusion

It is easy to see why there is a growing interest in the study of forgiveness. With so many positive effects, including being a pathway to deeper happiness, it is not surprising that it is being researched. Forgiveness has a relevance to all of our relationships. It has a significant part to play in our interactions at home or at work or among friends or between nations.

We have observed that it is not that easy to pursue and becomes even more difficult when someone acknowledges no wrongdoing on their part and refuses to accept our forgiveness or, if we have wronged them, offer us forgiveness. Yet it is a route worth taking. There is short-term pleasure in anger but potentially life-long pain in not embracing this change of mind and for that reason it is something worth being trained in.

Chapter 6

Invest time and energy in friends and family

Introduction

In the previous few chapters we have been trying to work out who the happiest people are that we know and what makes them so happy. As part of this, we also spent some time thinking about who the saddest people are that we know and why they are so miserable.

If we look at many of the films that have been released recently, the happiest people are those who are involved in some form of romantic relationship. Sure, the journey to discovering their true love is rather fraught, but once they finally find them then the last few minutes of the film suggest that their fate is to live happily ever after. It is in the spirit of this belief that so many magazines carry articles on finding the perfect partner or how to keep your mate.

Following those who find happiness in romantic love are those who are either given magical powers or find themselves caught up in some form of 'save the world from extinction' or 'good versus evil' plot. Admittedly, as with those in search of romantic love, you very rarely see a smile on their faces, yet within their intensity or innocent amazement and discovery there is that invisible and yet tangible joy. Maybe the answer to happiness is to find true love with someone who is on an adventure!

When we shrink this all down to our small world, then the people we know who are the happiest people and have been consistently so are those who are in meaningful relationships. These connections have mostly been with another human being, but occasionally with animals – like a pet they adore. The reverse is also true. The people we know who are possibly some of the most miserable people on the planet and have seemingly eternally been so are those who are in destructive marriages and relationships.

Two are better than one – the science

Returning to the writings of Solomon in the biblical book of Ecclesiastes, there is a saying that has proven to be the experience of most people: 'Two are better than one'. Recent experiments around the link between close connections with people and happiness reveal that this ancient piece of wisdom is in fact accurate. Meaningful relationships are the single most important human booster of happiness. Our friends are a more potent force for happiness than satisfaction with our job or healthy finances.

In her book *The How of Happiness*, Sonja Lyubomirsky states that 'relationships constitute the single most important factor responsible for the survival of *homo sapiens*'. This tallies with the research findings of Martin Seligman and Ed Diener, who observed that those with meaningful relationships were happier than those who did not have such networks.

It was the Roman statesman Cicero who said that 'to take friendship out of life is to take the sun away from the world'. Perhaps that is why in a survey that asked 'What was the last bad thing to happen to you?', over fifty per cent pointed to a relationship break-up or the loss of a friend.

Mother Teresa warned that the greatest epidemic in the world today is not leprosy or cancer, severe as they are, but rather loneliness. From the number of advertisements in the lonely hearts column it is obvious that this 'dis-ease' is at epidemic proportions. As Aristotle said, 'Without friends, no happiness is possible.'

In unpacking what meaningful relationships may look like, Lyubomirsky goes on to suggest that happy people are more likely to be married and have a fulfilling and long lasting relationship; they are more likely to be satisfied with their family life and social habits, more likely to consider their partner as their 'great love' and more likely to receive emotional and tangible support from friends, supervisors and co-workers. They are going to be people who are surrounded by meaningful relationships. These are relationships where there is unconditional love, meaning and pleasure.

Why are relationships so good for us? Very simply, they satisfy a number of deeply felt drives and they add significant dimensions to our lives. Whether it is as the older western tradition teaches that we were created that way or as some scientists would speculate that we have evolved in such a way, human beings are motivated by a desire to be in meaningful relationships. We connect with someone in order to procreate. Our bias is to stay in that relationship because we know it is the best environment within which to bring up our offspring. It has been shown that those who have no sense of belonging can suffer from different physical and mental challenges. It is because of these that we naturally find it difficult to break up with friends or a partner.

An added reason why relationships are so good for us relates to the support that we receive from them. Research conducted on three different continents among those communities that have elderly people living among them revealed that of the five things those elderly people had in common the foremost was that they were all socially engaged. It is from our relationships that we derive strength during life's most difficult times – how important were our friends during the loss of a job, a miscarriage, the death of our parents or, on a lighter note, when we stood on the scales and found out that we had put on four pounds in a week! There is no better known way of walking through life's hardest moments than in the company of a friend.

Next, relationships are good for us because they provide the means of giving us, and enabling us to express, the love that we crave. Love is the number one happiness-inducing emotion. There is a discussion to be had as to what type of love we are talking about. Although love includes romantic and sexual love, transforming love goes much deeper and flows wider than that and includes something of hope and meaning. When the Beatles sang, 'All we need is love', they were absolutely right.

A primary reason why relationships are important for us is that they provide and feed one of the few insatiable appetites that we have as we travel through life. In addition to seeking what Pascal called the 'God-shaped hole' that is inside each of us, we spend our lives in search of being able to love and be loved. Although we can find ourselves in deeply meaningful relationships, that thirst is never satisfied.

An advantage of having friends or a soul mate is that they provide us with what some people call a circle of creativity. In offering us security and acceptance they give us space to explore who we are and what we bring to this world.

Lastly, that which draws us to not giving up on people who fail us but which enchants us to move on is the way in which the company of friends colours life's experiences. With friends experiences are intensified, pain is consoled and moments of delight are deepened.

It is no wonder that the TV sitcom *Friends* was a hit for so long or that so many women want friends like Carrie, Samantha, Miranda or Charlotte from *Sex and the City*. Life is clearly richer in the company of others.

To join the dots, if the happiest people in the world are those with many good relationships and if from the experiments that have been conducted (and our own personal experience) it is apparent that quality relationships are good for you, then we have to take the time to invest in them. Having identified the people we have a special connection with then we should ensure that we implement a strategy for making these relationships better.

As we commit ourselves to nurturing our friendships we enter into something that psychologists call an upward spiral. Happy people have good friends. If these happy people invest in their relationships then they develop better friends. The presence of better friends in your life makes you happier. The happier you are the better quality of friends you attract and so on.

Marriage

Although what we have to say in this chapter is hopefully relevant to every relationship, we particularly want to focus on those who have entered into long-term partnerships whether married or not. To bring happiness into our relationships it's important to give particular focus on enjoying your life with your partner.

Marriage buffers us from the storms of life. It is the place where we experience the whole gambit of love – romantic, sexual, intimate and sacrificial. It is hard work and needs our full attention. Even though there are thousands of books on how to improve your relationship, today in the USA about forty per cent of those who marry will get divorced.

The statistics reveal that those with a deeply spiritual commitment are less likely to be divorced than those who have no such commitment. There are many who are convinced that marriage was designed by God to provide us with companionship and intimacy. The home should be a place of equality, solidity and liberty. It should be a place where everyone is safe. It can be pivotal to society. Marriage has the potential to give us life's greatest adventure.

Friendship

Contrary to our age of independence, people are in search of good friends. There are many advantages in having friends: Solomon said that with friends you can accomplish more, have someone to pick you up when you fall down, know companionship for the darkest time and that there is greater safety in numbers. Aristotle noted that it is the primary way of obtaining the virtuous life – a quality of character that is marked by courage, generosity and love. It seems that we need others in order to become all that we were created to be.

A friend is someone with whom you share something of your life – the greater the friend then the more you share. Deep friendship is like having another self!

Friendship is something that doesn't just happen but requires intentional effort over time. For Aristotle it is best begun when you see some quality in another that you admire. Friendship is developed when that is reciprocated.

Friendships can be formed because of a shared pleasure and because of a mutual usefulness but neither of these, in his mind, compares with a friendship based on character.

Perfect friendship is when your mate is focused on your welfare before their own. As Michael de Montaigne said, true friendship is when 'I give myself to my friend more than I seek to pull him to me'. We all know that it is when life is difficult that we discover who our friends are.

Steps to take

This attitude of being focused on the other rather than yourself is central to the teaching of the older western tradition about what characteristic should underscore all meaningful relationships. This 'household code', as it was termed by Martin Luther, with reference to what went on among the wider family, encouraged everyone to give themselves away for the good of the other. It's about focusing your life on the fulfilling of the other person's needs, which in turn leads to joy for working for the good of someone else.

So how do you go about developing deep and meaningful relationships? What follows is a long list – it's a menu for what you can try.

Develop daily rituals for partings and reunions

Gone are the days when a family would all have breakfast at the table and chat about the day ahead. However, there is great vitality in taking the time to find out at least one thing that will be going on in each other's lives during the day. If it is a friend then an occasional text or phone call will work a treat. It helps everyone appreciate that they are not alone and others are aware of what they are going through.

Concerning reunions, these need to be carefully guarded and unhurried moments when you get a chance to catch up on has gone on during the day or since the last time you saw each other. With long working days, possibly children and many demands on your time, a degree of creativity has to be used to find the space to re-connect. When away from family and friends, what about planning to regularly ring home or use email to stay in touch?

Share an inner life – walk with them in their garden

Everyone has an inner garden. It is a place where they walk and dream their dreams; a sacred space where they reflect on their goals, their fears, their hopes and their mistakes. Without doubt the number one way of investing time and energy into your very special relationships is to walk with someone in their garden. You will have to be invited, but if you are then there is a level of connection that takes place which creates the potential of soul mates. It is the place of life-long friends.

If as a married couple you are able to merge your inner gardens into one then it becomes the place from where you grow together, where you explore the future together, where you celebrate life's achievements and mourn life's losses. Lyubomirsky suggests that every week you need to do at least one thing that connects with your sacred place. This could include talking about the future or asking how things are going. It could be buying your friend a book on some aspect of their dreams.

Listen

Listening is an incredible aphrodisiac and therefore needs to be used wisely. The listening we are talking about here is more than simply hearing the words that are being spoken; it is hearing the deeper meaning contained in them and behind them. It is a form of listening that is in itself extremely tiring and yet deeply rewarding for the person speaking and the one listening. More often than not in conversation we are quiet as we wait for an opening to have our say. It is learning to share in the suspense of the one speaking. One of the problems that many teenagers have to work through (and some adults) is a poor self-image. The impact of friends who give others the time of day is deeply therapeutic.

Date

During the course of a relationship the time and day for connecting will change, but for those people who are married it is a good idea to plan to have when possible a weekly date. Spending money is not the issue; a little creativity will enable the most strapped-for-cash find ways to enjoy each other's company. There may need to be a little give and take on what you do. On some occasions indulge your partner by allowing them to completely plan the occasion.

Go on an adventure together

If you can't take a week off work or afford to go away, plan days out with those closest to you. Visit the museum or a local park. Go for a walk in a nearby forest. If money is not an issue, take someone to a special event and savour the experience together. Children remember days out more than we think they do and so do really good friends.

Cheer each other on

Those who walk in each other's garden want the best for each other. As such they are people who are always encouraging their partner or friend to be the best they can be. Believing that there is something beautiful in every person which needs to be drawn out, this is known as the 'Michelangelo effect'.

Make time

People have been getting better at the work–life balance. True, every now and then it goes out of the window, but generally we are all better at managing our time. What needs to follow is a wiser use of the time that we spend with those we love and care for.

Rather than sit in front of the TV for hours not talking to anyone, what about finding out what your children are doing and going and talking to them? If you are all watching something why not, at an appropriate moment, start a conversation about it?

Hug

Giving a hug is a great way of letting a close friend know that you love them. We all know people who just love to be hugged. For them there is nothing in the world like being engulfed by the person who loves them and wants to hold them tight.

Capitalize on good fortune

Friendships blossom when those around you take joy in each other's success.

Give spiritual input

In those families or friendships where there is a spiritual connection, take time to stimulate each other's spiritual quest. Go to a spiritual gathering together, perhaps read the Bible and pray together. Ask each other's opinion about issues. Establish an environment where you can explore the spiritual and how it impacts your lives.

Manage conflict

There are arguments in every relationship. Handled properly they offer the opportunity for a greater connection – and the fun of making up. But there are hazards that need to be avoided. There is a conversation going on at the moment around the idea that men and women argue differently. An illustration of this could be in how women often want to talk about an issue but men go into a stony silence. Research conducted by Elaine D. Eater found that more men than women have a tendency to bottle up their feelings. In response to those who want to magnify a difference in the way that the sexes argue, Deborah Cameron suggests that 'the idea that men and women differ fundamentally in the way they use language to communicate is a myth'. Whether that is true or not there are elements that you don't want to find in any type of heated conversation.

We are going to look at how to handle a time of conflict well later on in the chapter, but for now let's identify the characteristics of a destructive conversation. What are they? Harmful conversations normally begin with a harsh interchange of accusation and sarcasm. This is followed by a form of criticism which moves on from the point of debate and attacks the character of the other person involved in what now feels like a war. After this comes contempt – this can include rolling the eyes or a look of disgust. Then comes a defensive stance – 'It's not my problem, it is you; you are the one to blame.' Lastly there is some form of stonewalling as it becomes clear that the other person is not listening. It could include the person walking from the room.

Be loyal

That sense that your friend is always going to stand up for you – and when they think you are wrong chat with you in private about it – is so attractive. To have someone in your life whom you know you can trust with every secret is calming and liberating.

Forgive

As we discovered in the last chapter there is incredible power in forgiveness. A serious effort must be made to place this as one of the central values of your closest relationships. How many marriages have been soured by one partner failing to offer forgiveness to the other? How many siblings have grown apart while still living under the same roof because they never learned to forgive the other for their foolish, selfish and stupid actions?

Support

We all need support at times during our lives. This attitude wherein you aim to be there when your friend needs you adds great value to a friendship. It is important to remember calendar dates that have significant meaning for your friend, and to be contactable when you know they are going to be facing an appraisal at work or have to attend a difficult meeting. If one of their parents is unwell then be sure to keep an extra eye on them.

Empathize

We all find it easier to connect with those we think know what we are going through. Take time to be with those who are hurting.

Appreciate

Some people find it very easy to nag, to always see the negative in every situation. Research has shown that in relationships where there is a five to one ratio of positive to negative comments: those relationships flourish. It is important to consider the difficulties of a situation and to be (negatively) encouraged to change yourself or the situation in some way, but better still are the positive encouragements of someone else. As we discovered in chapter 1, one of the ways to appreciate another person is by writing gratitude letters and then reading them to the person. Taking five minutes a day to express your appreciation can transform a person's life.

Give affection

It has to be appropriate to the person, the location and the nature of your relationship, but relationships thrive with affection. It can be verbal, physical or expressed with gifts. We all like to experience the love that someone has for us.

Be honest about imperfections

It is not uncommon in family life for someone to have a 'perfect moment' – an occasion when they pontificate about the rightness or wrongness of somebody's actions while forgetting about their own imperfections. Something that helps when these moments occur is an openness in the family to label it for what it is.

Certainly such honesty needs to be appropriate and wisely shared, but how formative for everyone else in the family to know that you don't have to pretend to be what you are not. In acknowledging our weakness we are not suggesting that that is the end of the story but rather a starting point for a conversation about how that person may be able to move on or at least cope with that particular aspect of their character or consequence of their action.

Be intimate

We all have a desire to be known. Picking up on some of the pointers that we have given in this section, take time to discover the journey that your friends are on. Every now and then ask them where they are on that journey.

Speak the language of love

The respected marriage and family life expert, Dr Gary Chapman, identified that there are five languages of love. They are words, actions, time, gifts and touch. It is very important that we figure out what language it is that our partner speaks. It could save us from an awful lot of heartache and expense! If their love language is different from that of our parents then we will not have any role model to fall back on. If it is different from ours then we stand a chance of always failing to communicate what we want to. We may think we are expressing the fact that we love them but it may be in a way that they cannot understand.

115

Reminisce

One evening during a staff get-together conversation turned to how the various people present had met their partner. It was hilarious and a little too scary to discover how each person had begun to flirt with their partner, what qualities they had seen, the fears they had had and where life had taken them. But what a deeply enriching evening, both for those who told their story and for those who listened. Taking time to reminisce, as we discovered when we looked at savouring life's joys, is an exercise that brings so much pleasure and it is something that can greatly benefit relationships.

When Patrick and Elizabeth got married, one of their friends was invited to speak at the wedding ceremony. The guest speaker made three simple points. First, life will change and some of these changes will be planned, while others cannot be controlled. Second, life will get difficult at times – in fact there will be moments when both parties will be overwhelmed by life's issues. Third, time should be taken to develop deep roots because it is these that will hold couples close and upright during those moments. The list we have just looked at here represents some of the many ways in which we dig deep roots in our relationships.

Managing conflict

'And they all lived happily ever after', is a misnomer for married life. They might well have walked off into the sunset, but it is pretty definite that there were more than a few squabbles as they set about cultivating a home for themselves and any children that might follow. The mistaken notion that finding true love in some way guarantees eternal bliss is a dangerous lie.

Married life is a landscape for skirmishes. Sonja Lyubomirsky notes how 'happy couples don't necessarily fight any less or any less loudly, they just fight differently'. That is why the best thing that someone about to get married can do is enrol in some form of conflict resolution class. When most couples argue, more often than not they follow the example that has been set them by their parents, whether that example was helpful or not! Some take the Eskimo approach: they freeze the other person out of the relationship; some take the gunfighter stance: firing negative remarks at their partner; some attempt the great escape: they try and disappear from the room; and some play Jekyll and Hyde: they turn dangerously violent.

In their book *Making Love Last*, Bill and Lynne Hybels offer their six-step plan for how to have a good healthy argument and then move on. It isn't rocket science but it is a helpful guide.

Pray about it

As Christians, prayer is a very important part of Bill and Lynne's married life. Consequently they consider it vital that every day they ask God to protect and stimulate their marriage and, when there is a heated conversation brewing, that he show them where they are personally at fault. Whatever you think about the place of prayer, you have to admire the wisdom of taking a breather from the conflict to reflect.

Plan a peace conference

This is the heart of their process. They suggest five rooms into which they must walk as they work through any issue. It is an unwritten rule that they will hold this conference as soon as possible, when it is mutually convenient and after they have both adequately prepared for it. As they wait to begin their discussions they commit themselves to not taking pot shots at each other.

a. Begin with affirmation – take a few minutes to speak positive words into each other's lives.

b. Be willing to take the blame – there is incredible power in saying 'I'm sorry'.

c. Express hurt rather than hostility – we all get hurt, we all hurt those closest to us. To feel hurt is a legitimate emotion. However, what we have to ensure is that we do not allow that feeling to turn into anger.

d. Make 'I feel' statements – it is very easy to turn the conversation into a blaming session. What is important is that you express your point of view but not accuse them of failing – even if they have.

e. Avoid 'never' and 'always' – beware of extremes.

Added to this could be: identify what it is that you are fighting about, know if your argument is worth it, make sure that you listen to what the other person is saying, do not interrupt, be considerate, acknowledge their perspective, appropriately use friendly humour, try not to swear too much, keep your voice at a normal level and know when to walk away for now.

Be solution centred

Since they come into these discussions with a spirit of reconciliation they are working towards finding a solution. There may be a compromise, they may have to adjust or adapt. They are looking for a win-win ending.

Ensure there is a moment of truth

Although committed to resolution they are not prepared to devalue the importance of the issue and therefore if no satisfactory outcome can be achieved they will commit themselves to coming back to the issue after they have given it some more personal thought and more conversation together.

Seek the counsel of friends if it is needed

Bill and Lynne are not foolish enough to think that they have the answers for every issue that they face. Therefore, they are open to the idea of seeking the wise counsel of friends. In the book, Bill notes how on occasion he may go and chat with someone privately or Bill and Lynne may even go together.

Consider professional help

In some cultures nothing is thought of going and asking for professional advice and yet in others it is a stigma that keeps people from receiving the help they so desperately need.

There are no guarantees that marriage will work, as we have already noted, and for many it does not. As we think about investing time and energy in our relationship, one of the keys to reaping the benefits of that is having an idea of what to do when we fall out with the people we love.

Chapter 7

Take care of your body and soul

Introduction

It can be easy to lose sight of who we are. Having lived abroad as a result of his job, Jim recently moved back home, and with the stress of buying a new house and settling into a new job he felt that he had lost sight of who he was. But, with the help of a couple of old friends and having begun to settle into a bit of a routine, Jim now believed that he was beginning to get back to being his old self.

The idea of losing sight of who you are is a familiar tale. It is told by people who have been married for a number of years – or pre-occupied with rearing their children or consumed by their career – and then suddenly wake up to the fact that there is more to life. It is one of those mini-crises that hang around the bigger question of personal identity that we sometimes ask as, 'Who am I?'

This core question of self-knowledge drives many of the social sciences today. In addition to the cosmologist wanting to understand how our universe works and the biologist the origin of our species, psychologists want to understand why we behave in the way that we do. It has always been one of the most fascinating questions. Today it is in vogue because with the downgrading of history (now seen as the telling of the winner's tale and not necessarily a true recital of the facts), the weakening of objective truth (there are truths about our world that are now negotiable) and a growing interest in our private inner world, we have turned our attention inwards and want greater clarity on our internal make-up.

As experienced by Matt Damon's character, Jason Bourne, in the film *Bourne Identity*, in being awakened to the fact that we are not just the physical body inside the clothes we are wearing, we find ourselves surrounded by many competing voices offering us their take on our identity: the job centre that wants to label our skills, the beautician who wants to clarify our age and the quality of our skin and then the products that we need to purchase, and the relationship counsellor who wants to offer us various programmes for our roles as child, parent, partner, sibling, employer, employee, uncle/auntie and friend. Shops on the High Street want us to believe that we are where we shop, the clothes that we buy and the bags that we carry them home in. But surely we are more than this!

Body and soul

A group of churches recently ran a 'mind, body and soul' stall at their local town summer festival. Of all the 'tables' at the jamboree this was possibly one of the most popular stopping places. As well as offering face painting for the kids, and hand massage and other body-enhancing goodies for the adults, they also dedicated a section of their stall to offering an 'à la carte' menu of spiritual practices and commodities that would help people on their spiritual journey. Perhaps one of the most exciting elements of their 'body and soul' ensemble was their offering to pray for people, laying on their hands and asking for spiritual and physical healing.

This idea of linking the body and soul together and caring for them both is no longer that rare. Over recent years there has been an enormous growth in this type of fair – driven by a deep longing to encounter the spiritual in life. Most quality magazines have sections entitled 'body and soul'. What is actually understood by 'body and soul' is normally a little hazy, but it does highlight a re-awareness that we are far more than just a physical body.

In this chapter we aim to explore how we go about caring for our soul. We will make a slight detour to keep the *Vogue* readers of this world happy and comment on caring for our body too. But, with so much having been written on how to care for your body, we thought that a better use of space would be to rummage in the often confusing, neglected and undervalued area of soul care. Both body and soul are important to happiness, and neither should be neglected.

We'll get down to the nitty gritty of offering a possible definition of what we mean by the soul later. Suffice it to say that we will be looking at the spiritual dimension of the soul. However, before we do that we want to set a context for our conversation.

In making a distinction between body and soul we are not suggesting that they should be seen as disconnected in any way. It is purely for simplicity as we look at how we go about caring for each that they have been highlighted separately. In attempting to categorize the needs that we have, Abraham Maslow identified that there was integration between the spiritual and the biological within each of us. The spirit life is part of our biological life. It may be a higher and more important element than the physical, yet it is a part of it. To be human is to be a spiritual being. It is part of the real self, of one's inner being. For those from the older western tradition it is understood as that which God breathed into the first human to make living beings – it is the divine breath within us – which makes us who we are.

As we noted above, whereas the major focus has been on caring for the physical element of our being, today that is gradually changing and with people becoming more aware that they are as much spiritual beings as physical beings a conversation has begun on how we care for our spirit as well as our body.

Taking care of your body

The basic argument is simple. Our bodies have needs that we must work at meeting. As they are met so we increase the potential for happiness. Of course, not all of our needs are to do with our external bodies. What takes place inside of us with regard to our emotional health is also important.

An experiment was conducted with a group of people who all suffered from depression. One section of the group was given an exercise programme to follow, another section a course of tablets to take and the third section was given both. At the end of the experiment, the results showed that all three groups had exhibited improvement in their mental health. Physical exercise was good for them. What is more, the SMILE project, as it became known, reported that after several months those who had done the physical exercise had retained a degree of happiness.

Why should exercise have this impact? The idea that exercise has a beneficial impact on mood and a sense of well-being is confirmed by many research studies. The unique contribution of the SMILE project was to demonstrate that exercise is not just marginally beneficial but is at least as helpful as the taking of the well-known antidepressant that was used as part of this experiment. In addition, it is worth stressing that exercise does not have harmful side effects and is very cost effective. Nor does the exercise taken need to be beyond the reach of ordinary people. Even older people who had lived somewhat sedentary lives were able to walk briskly for twenty to thirty minutes several times a week and achieve the same helpful results.

May there be some factors at work here beyond the purely physical? It is possible that there is a benefit in committing to something that is structured and regular. We may gain a sense of well-being or achievement simply by engaging in an activity that we have set as a goal. We may well feel that we have contributed to our own well-being and the knowledge that we have some element of contribution to improved health or even control over our lives may act as its own reward leading to positive feelings. Research around the psychological factors beyond the purely physical benefits of exercise continues.

Steps to take: looking after your body

How else may you care for your body? There is a good deal of evidence to suggest that when we feel good about ourselves we take care of our appearance. Healthy self-love causes us to present ourselves well. The converse follows. When we do not feel we are worthy of being loved then we cease to think about the way we look. Making a positive self-affirmation of our personal worth can be reinforced by taking time to think about our bodies. The following can help.

Take time to feel good about your physical appearance. Plan a regular slot to soak in the bath, get your hair cut, trim your beard, moustache or side-burns, cut your nails, preen and pluck, bleach or wax, apply your face mask and paint your nails. And don't forget to shop for clothes.

Evidence from surveys suggests that men are somewhat less interested in paying attention to their personal appearance than women but this could be changing. One survey suggested that one in ten men aged eighteen to fifty is already on the 'cutting edge' in terms of thinking about their appearance. Seventy-five per cent of this group of men use facial moisturizers and seventy per cent in the same group buy tailored clothes and have manicures or pedicures.

Apparently, half of all men are open to using such products in the future but still forty-three per cent of men are described as 'low maintenance'; that is, they confine their personal grooming to shower, shave and aftershave. Two-thirds of men say the reason for this is that they don't have the time – which may be another way of saying that it's not high on their personal agenda.

So, without going overboard, it is possible to invest some time in personal appearance. Think about your wardrobe, figure out what colours you look best in. Check out your physical condition with a simple health check. See if you may need to lose a little weight and work out a very basic routine to do that. Consider some regular physical exercise.

Sleep

Try to regularly get good quality sleep. The question of sleeping well has become an issue in modern life. The invention of artificial light has offered humankind the option of distorting or extending the natural day. Try living in a society where electricity is not available and you will find that your natural rhythm of waking and sleeping is shaped much more around the actual hours of daylight. Industrialization has produced shift working, while more recent developments such as twenty-four-hour TV and the use of the Internet push us towards a lifestyle in which sleep becomes an intrusion.

The relationship between sleeping well and overall health is still controversial as a subject, but health specialists are increasingly pointing to research that connects good sleep (which includes enough sleep) with overall patterns of health. Being awake in the early hours of the morning runs counter to the body's internal clock, throwing a host of bodily functions out of sync. 'Lack of sleep disrupts every physiological function in the body,' says Eve Van Cauter of the University of Chicago. 'We have nothing in our biology that allows us to adapt to this behavior.'

How much sleep is enough? Clearly the answer to that question does vary from person to person, but the norm is between seven and nine hours. It is not a coincidence that sleep deprivation is used in interrogation techniques and can be classified as torture. So how do you help yourself to get a better night's sleep? The National Sleep Foundation offers the following ten tips:

1. Maintain a regular bedtime and waketime schedule, including at weekends.

2. Establish a relaxing bedtime routine, such as soaking in a hot bath or hot tub and then reading a book or listening to soothing music.

3. Create a sleep-conducive environment that is dark, quiet, comfortable and cool.

4. Sleep on a comfortable mattress and pillow.

5. Use your bedroom only for sleep and sex. It is best to take work materials, computers and TVs out of the sleeping environment.

6. Finish eating at least two to three hours before your regular bedtime.

7. Exercise regularly. It is ideal to complete your workout at least a few hours before bedtime.

8. Avoid alcohol, nicotine (e.g., cigarettes, tobacco products), and caffeine (e.g., coffee, tea, soft drinks, chocolate) close to bedtime. These can lead to poor sleep, keep you awake or disrupt sleep later in the night.

9. We all know the importance of eating well. Ensure that you regularly get your quota of fruit and veg. With that it is crucial that you drink as much water as you need. Work towards your ideal weight. We all have a set point. And as we have already noted, get regular exercise in a form that is appropriate for you. If you are too busy to exercise, you are too busy.

10. Work with your partner to have good and satisfying sex.

Sex

The often neglected but necessary ingredients of sex are those of communication and self-giving. Talk to your partner about what they like and what they don't and attempt to satisfy their needs before your own. With both of you looking to give the other person a really good time it should last longer than the average five minutes. It remains a curious fact that we live in a society that bombards us with sexual images and there's a good deal of conversation about sex and yet (and perhaps partly because of this bombardment) we are deeply anxious about the subject of sex. The issue is not the amount of sexual activity but the difference between healthy and unhealthy sex. One model to help us think about healthy sex is the CERTS model: Consent, Equality, Respect, Trust and Safety.

- **CONSENT** means you can freely and comfortably choose whether or not to engage in sexual activity. You are able to stop the activity at any time during the sexual contact.

- **EQUALITY** means your sense of personal power is on an equal level with your partner. Neither of you dominates the other.

- **RESPECT** means you have positive regard for yourself and for your partner. You feel respected by your partner.

- **TRUST** means you trust your partner on both a physical and an emotional level. You have mutual acceptance of vulnerability and an ability to respond to it with sensitivity.

- **SAFETY** means you feel secure and safe within the sexual setting. You are comfortable with and assertive about where, when and how the sexual activity takes place. You feel safe from the possibility of harm, such as unwanted pregnancy, sexually transmitted infection and physical injury.

What is important is that we appreciate the responsibility that we have to honour and care for our body. We have to be careful not to abuse it or to see it as our ultimate concern. As those who are as much soul as body we need to focus on both. This is particularly difficult in a culture that is over-focused on the body beautiful and where your sense of self-worth, the response of others and on occasion career advancement can be based on your looks alone.

Taking care of your soul

When it comes to defining what we mean by caring for our soul, spiritual and character formation guru Dallas Willard suggests that it is caring for the inner stream that runs from the core of our being through all that we are. Our soul is our centre, the uniqueness that defines who we are.

As we noted earlier, there is a spiritual dimension to our soul and it is when this spiritual essence connects with the divine life that we begin to experience the flowing of fresh and invigorating living water in this inner stream. To push this 'stream' metaphor a little further, the older western tradition paints a picture of humankind as those who have been contaminated over time – things didn't go as they were meant to at the point of humankind's origin and we have been suffering the consequences of it ever since. The pollution isn't so bad that we don't still see a reflection of the breath of God within us, but it is not as good as it was originally intended to be.

It is for that reason that many spiritual writers refer to the soul as a battlefield where there is a war between our original image and the one that has been contaminated – think good angel and little devil sitting one on each shoulder egging you on. Now, there is a conversation to be had as to what reconnecting with the spiritual may mean. Some people see the spiritual as a searching after the sacred (the divine something or other that is out there). Others search for the spiritual in religion and others look to take spiritual components and apply them to their lives without rooting them in any divine force or structure: they see work as a calling, marriage as a sacrament and children as a blessing.

Many have found help in this complex area by connecting these disciplines to the very attractive example of Jesus. Without some clear rooting we can be in danger of becoming aware of the spiritual world and possibly having some experiences of it without being able to draw on its real benefit. It's a bit like trying to eat chocolate without knowing how to take the wrapper off. Getting inside to get at the really good stuff is important.

The science of a spirit life

It is a recognized truth that those who invest in their spiritual life are happier than those who do not. In fact, research also confirms that those with a spiritual life are also physically healthier than those who neglect this part of their being.

Research has revealed that people with some form of faith (normally Judeo-Christian, since it is the most researched to date) recover better from trauma, adjust more easily to physically challenging illnesses, live longer and are generally more healthy. On one level this more attractive quality of life is due to the healthier behaviours that they engage in as part of their faith outlook, the deeper and wider social networks that they are involved in and their sense of identity that comes as being part of such groups.

And yet this is not the whole picture, for as Sonja Lyubomirsky wisely observes, people with faith claim to have a personal connection with a loving and caring God who takes care of them, brings meaning to their lives so that the most mundane of activities is made sacred and encourages them into activities that are themselves happiness boosters – gratitude, forgiveness and practising kindness to name but a few.

Those with a working spirituality are not immune to the difficult and even tragic times of life, but they go through such with companionship and a belief that there is meaning to it even if they never figure out what that explanation is this side of eternity. What is more, as part of a spiritual community that has gratitude as one of its defining characteristics, there is a growing bias within them to be thankful.

Steps to take: spiritual disciplines

Spiritual disciplines act as companions for the journey. They all have the potential to help us reconnect with the spirit life that is outside of ourselves. They can be welcomed as forms of training that help us to observe and practise our spiritual life. Like learning any new skill they can seem rather awkward and a little strange at first, but gradually, like a new hairstyle or a pair of rugby boots, everything finally sits comfortably.

They enable us to make space for the divine spark that burns in our lives. Many people have very busy lives any awareness of the spiritual reality that is all around us is quickly lost as we think about getting people ready for school, going to work, actioning all of the points on our to do list, attending meetings, travelling home, eating and trying to catch up with our family. Spiritual disciplines, if carefully and regularly scheduled into our week, give us the option of obtaining spiritual refreshment.

Dallas Willard divides his list of spiritual disciplines into two groups: those he labels as 'disciplines of abstinence', which he believes refine the drives of the body which may crowd out any searching after the spiritual, and 'disciplines of engagement', which aim to bring something of the divine back into our most sacred place. In his abstinence grouping he includes solitude, silence, fasting, frugality, chastity (there was a great article recently about how a thirty-day fast from sex saved someone's marriage.[6] Not for everyone,

6 The article was based on the book Sex Detox by Dr Ian Kerner. Published by HarperCollins, 2008.

but if employed wisely it definitely has the potential of rekindling passion), secrecy and sacrifice. In the engaging group he includes study, worship, celebration, service, prayer, fellowship, confession and submission.

The actual list of possible disciplines which you can try out as you look to develop your spiritual life is endless. For in addition to those mentioned above, there is also voluntary exile, holding a vigil, journaling, Sabbath keeping and physical exercise. It's worth looking at a few of these in a little more detail. For those wanting to get on and have a go, we suggest that you gradually work through the list picking a couple at a time. Some are going to be fun and some not (depending on temperament), some easy to access and others painfully difficult. Once you've given all a try or at least thought about doing them all, then you will be in a place to focus in on those that suit you.

Prayer

It seems that a great number of people pray already. It is reported that seven out of ten Americans pray on a daily basis and a similar number in the UK. The core of prayer is the idea of a spiritual conversation taking place between us and God. Depending on the closeness of our relationship with him, we either talk to him as one of his creation or as a child to a parent. As in all mature conversations prayer is not only a matter of speaking to God but also of taking the time to listen for him to speak to us. The ways through which he does that could include life's unfolding events, the comments of friends or an internal sense of what is right. Those from the older western tradition would also want to include what we discover as we read the Bible.

Try taking a few minutes (to begin with) at the start and end of the day, or any other time you find easier for you, and dedicate that time on a regular basis to talk to God. This can be followed by spontaneously mentioning things to God that come up during the day. Thinking about the content of chapter 1 of 'Count your blessings', what about having a little blessing prayer that you say before you enjoy something special such as a meal, a concert or some time with very special friends? Many have found it useful to learn the Lord's Prayer and recite it at the start of each day. We can use it as a launch pad to pray for other things.

When it comes to what to include in your prayers, anything goes. You can talk to God about your day, mention issues that concern you about your family, friends or work. If after watching the news on TV you are concerned about some political situation in this country or around the world then you can talk to God about that.

It's important to know that prayer is not something that you just do on your knees or in church on a Sunday, and that when it comes to answering prayer God answers every single prayer that we pray, though wisely not always with a yes!

Meditation

In the older western tradition meditation is not about emptying your mind but rather filling it
with thoughts about spiritual truth as found in its sacred text, the Bible. Rather than attempting to detach our minds from our circumstances this meditative practice is about exploring the meaning of the text and applying it to the situation that we find ourselves in.

With a motivation to feed our soul the aim of this type of meditation is to listen to God speak to us through his word. To meditate means to chew the cud – to put it through the washing machine of your mind and draw from it the life it contains – to turn it over in your mind again and again.

As for how to meditate, this is best learned on the job. The skill is to cultivate your attention, which only really comes with practice. However, some pointers are useful for those starting out.

If it is possible to memorize the section that you are thinking about all the better, as this facilitates the option of returning to your thoughts again and again throughout the day. If you are able to remember particular passages then you can play with them in your mind in all sorts of locations.

Any meditation should be enveloped by a short prayer for help in the process and then thanks for insights gained afterwards. It is helpful to find a comfortable place that is as free as possible from distractions. In many senses posture is a personal preference but many people find sitting comfortably with a straight back with their eyes closed, gently breathing in and out helps.

Once a sense of stillness has been achieved, the idea then is to use your mind to understand the text. This includes questioning what is there: imagining what it would have been like to have been there, perhaps thinking about how that would work out in your life. There is no doubt that your mind will wander again and again from what you are trying to do. When that happens, gently draw your attention back to the task in hand. We are aiming to engage in an unhurried act of thoughtful reflection on a spiritual text. In a world of busyness that is going to be a challenge.

For those for whom this exercise simply isn't them, what about taking the text, writing it in the centre of a piece of paper and after enveloping the exercise with prayer (as noted above), pick up a pen and doodle around what the text may mean and how it could be relevant for you?

Retreats

It takes most people a little while to appreciate the benefit of taking time out to go on retreat. With such busy lives we often feel that we don't have enough time to stop what we are doing and take time off to go in search of God. At its most basic level a retreat is carving out in your diary a period of time when you step out of your normal routine, physically travel to a different location and spend a quality period of time seeking after God.

For some people their retreat takes place in their garden or at a local park or on a favourite walk; for others it takes place in one of the many retreat houses that are found in many countries across the world.

Finding a soul friend

A soul friend is like having your own spiritual guide as a mate. It's an individual who walks with you through your spiritual journey. This is the person you can talk to about how you are getting on in your spiritual journey, issues that you are struggling with or successes that you are enjoying. Depending on the nature of the relationship, they may be able to suggest ways that you could move forward in your journey, possible books to read or disciplines to try. During a difficult period you could ask them to hold you accountable for your actions. What is important, as we identified when we looked at thanking a mentor, is that you think carefully about the person you want to be your soul friend or mentor. What qualities are you looking for? What is it about their life that attracts you to them?

Joining a group

As we noted above there is real benefit in belonging to a group that is on the same spiritual journey as you and is are kind and caring. This is a good opportunity to think more deeply about your journey, to chat with others and to laugh about all the things you are exploring. If you're not keen on going along to church this Sunday why not think about signing up for a locally run spiritual programme?[7]

Laughter

One of the disciplines missing on most lists is that of laughter. It belongs to a stream of spiritual activities that include being joyful, feasting, celebrating, partying or playfulness. It is that side of the spiritual life that is often neglected because it is seen as being of less value than the more sober disciplines which are most often called to mind.

Solomon comments in his wisdom that there is a time to laugh. He went on to say that one of the ways of living life in the midst of its realities (we are all going to die, life is a game of chance and that evil and insanity reside in the human heart) was that we were to 'always be dressed in white'. Which was his way of saying that we should always have our party clothes on. Whatever life throws at you, whatever you go through, learn to do internal aerobics – learn to laugh.

Today, the wisdom of Solomon's words endorsed by the medical profession which has no problem in listing the number of benefits of chuckling – reduction in stress hormones, improved circulation and the exercising of muscles – it is one of the proven ways to happiness. As we set about nurturing our soul we should remember that laughter is one of the key components.

---

7 For suggestions, see the Appendix 2 on page 157.

Fasting

As well as being physically beneficial when done properly, the spiritual discipline of fasting is an expression of someone's desire to create space to meet with God. This act of abstinence and self-denial opens up a window in the soul to engage more deeply with God. Acknowledging that fasting is not only to be connected with going without food for one meal but can also include giving up TV for an hour or not playing on the computer for a couple of hours, a weekly fast can make room for a more intense time of prayer or meditation. It very clearly sends the signal that this is important for you.

Nurturing a worldview

Australian psychologist Hugh McKay commented that we all have a particular way of looking at and interacting with the world that we live in. Often called a worldview, this belief structure gives explanation and meaning to everything that goes on around us. It shapes our value system, our view of suffering and how we perceive the future.

Many people have never taken the time to sketch out on a piece of paper their outlook on life, even less considered how the spiritual life interacts with this. Re-drawing your understanding of the big picture is no easy feat and very careful decisions have to be made on where you go to receive input. Taking fifteen minutes a day to read the Bible or some other spiritual book and then reflect upon what was read is a good way of beginning to think your way into how you could, should or do look at the world.

Service

Some of us are made in such a way that we find it easier to connect with God when we are serving others than when we are in a group chatting about spiritual issues or on our own with a book or saying a prayer or listening to a spiritual CD. There are a couple of reasons why this may be true. First, the God who made the earth joins us in our activity and so we sense his nearness and delight. Second, because we have learned to meet God in the people we are serving. A strange but incredibly motivating idea that has been around for at least a couple of thousand years, is that in caring for others we meet and serve the God who made them.

Being still with God

Modelled in the seventeenth century by the practically minded French monk Brother Lawrence, the idea is to so make sensitive your spiritual antenna that you are able to know and enjoy the presence of God wherever you are. Component parts of this discipline include remembering God throughout the day, learning to still the busyness of your mind and focus on the fact that God is everywhere and therefore where you are right now, admiring him and stilling your inner being. It may help to choose a single place where you grapple with this discipline and then try another and so on.

Conclusion

When people discover a new way forward, most want to master the path as quickly as possible. They want to get rich quick, shrink a dress or jeans size and win people over in four easy steps.

When it comes to engaging in the resourcing of our soul, the disciplines that make it possible take time to master and demand effort. The promise for those who are prepared to pay the price of training in them is a flourishing soul and so a happy heart.

Chapter 8

Develop strategies for coping with stress and hardships

Introduction

Sometimes she can be the life and soul of the party. A highly successful saleswoman, Valerie is known for being a bit of a giggle and it is not unusual to find her at the centre of whatever is going on. People seem to really like her. It is not uncommon for staff at the various shops she visits to tell her their life story. There is something about her that makes almost complete strangers feel comfortable when they whisper their secrets to her.

What almost nobody knows is that the outward expressions of competency, sociability, humour and perfect preening are only part of the picture. On the inside this late forty-something is in a mess. Two difficult teenagers, a long-standing physical ailment and an unsociable husband have meant that for the last sixteen years Valerie's inner world has been one of destructive turmoil. With no strength to honestly face the pain or causes of her deep unhappiness she has developed a number of instant, superficial and temporary coping reactions to whatever the latest emergencies are.

Her portfolio of responses to stressful moments includes stuffing herself with junk food (this normally kicks off the cycle of feeling bloated and then taking laxatives), consuming far more alcohol than she should, going on spending sprees or impulse buying, keeping herself busy at work or church, going quiet and/or storming out of the house.

For several years she has been a bit of a flirt. It has never been that serious but has just been enough to spike her life with some daring excitement.

Unfortunately, denial, avoidance, escapism, negative self-talk and pretence mean that happiness is a commodity that Valerie very rarely owns. Her set point for happiness is pretty much at the same level as everyone else's, but the negative emotional blanket of home along with the lack of an efficient strategy for coping with all the heartbreak in her life means that it's very rare for her to smile on the inside.

The battlefield

At some point or other everyone's life sucks. The possible causes can range from being caught up in traffic when you need to be at the school gate to pick up your daughter – to having a new boss who tells you that your face no longer fits in the team – to the discovery of a lump which is diagnosed as an aggressive form of cancer. There are some people for whom life always seems to suck.

In our context of finding out how we can be happier, the comment that most people make is 'How can I be expected to be happier when all this rubbish is going on in my life?' It is one of the biggest obstacles that people have to embracing more of the happy life – how do they cope with the stress and hardships that are part of being alive? In reality, there are steps that you can take to cope with the difficulties that life can throw at you. In fact, it is possible to have lots of miserable things happen to you and still become happier.

It is clearly not going to be easy – there is no bagging a bargain here – it is going to require a very concerted effort to track down and use these life-enhancing skills. When finding ourselves in a place of hardship, there are normally three possible outcomes to what we are going through – we can survive it, recover from it or thrive because of it. None of these outcomes are set in stone. They are all consequences of how we approach or think about our lives, what the reserves are that we have inside us and how we react to that which we find ourselves caught up in – and that's without thinking about whether we are optimists or pessimists!

The key to all this is to ensure that there are more positive thoughts and emotions than there are negative thoughts and emotions. That whatever our set point of happiness is, we are utilizing coping strategies to ensure that, if at all possible, when tough times come our way, we have the means to stop them from making us emotionally bankrupt.

Problem-focused and emotion-focused coping

When crisis a comes, we all respond to it in different ways – even when it is the same traumatic event. Some become fearful, others angry, a few are filled with guilt and some with disbelief. Then there is denial, shock and stress.

Psychology identifies two main routes that people take to deal with problems. Many of us, particularly men, attempt to cope with whatever is happening by engaging in a problem-solving approach. The way of dealing with the situation is to see how they can sort it out.

The idea is to obtain as much information about what is going on as possible and then to form a plan of action to deal with the difficulties. It is about dealing with the issue and not the effects of it. Part of the process could include learning a new skill, practising self-control or engaging in some form of confrontation.

This 7C action-based approach could have the following ingredients:

- Call the problem by its name

- Clarify what would take the problem away

- Consider all of the possible options for dealing with the issue

- Choose a particular route for dealing with the problem

- Calculate what could happen, the risks and the outcomes

- Carry out the plan

- Contemplate what happened. Did it solve the problem?

When the problem-solving approach fails or doesn't address the issue on its own, we join with those whose first response at coping is to do so emotionally. This is about reducing the symptoms of stress or the particular crisis that we are involved in.

There are lots of emotion-focused approaches that people call on. They are grouped predominantly into two categories: behavioural strategies (ways of acting) and cognitive strategies (different ways of thinking). As for adopting particular actions, these could include becoming engrossed in a meaningful project so as to distract us from what is going on, seeking emotional support or doing something that will give us a breather from the situation.

For many psychologists, the more interesting response is that of how people can and do change their thinking. Particular options include positively reinterpreting the situation, acceptance and embracing the spiritual as a positive affirmation of life.

Steps to take – strategies for coping

It is impossible to be too specific when you draw up a list of ways to cope. With so many different coping situations to be faced, there is no way that you can offer a catch-all list. There may be some similarities to how you go about coping with grief, exams, violence, affairs, cancer, flying and an intense sporting moment, but there are also significant differences.

Do all the things already mentioned in the book

If, at its crudest level, being happier is about so balancing the books that we have far more happy emotions and thoughts than negative ones, then it stands to reason that ensuring that we engage in the various ideas already noted in this book should help us during the darker times.

People who count their blessings, practise acts of kindness, savour life's joys, thank their mentors, learn to forgive, invest time and energy in family and friends and look after their body are storing up for themselves emotional capital.

Those who tackle difficult issues from a place of happiness think differently (and better) than those who do so from the place of sadness or misery. It seems that working on our happiness now not only puts smiles away for a rainy day but will also put us in the best frame of mind for tackling problems when they come.

Call on friends

In Genesis, the first book of the Bible, it is reported that God announced that it was not good for an individual to be alone. Psychological research would add that that is particularly the case during periods of stress or trauma. Of all the coping mechanisms that we can take up this is regarded as being the big one. People with a good support structure are less negatively affected by distressing situations than those without friends. Strangely it is often unused by those who find themselves in a crisis!

There are many benefits of having developed a good support structure around you. Relationships give you a place to belong, room to share your feelings, an opportunity to discover that you are not alone and the potential of seeing things differently – there will always be one of your friends who can see the other side of the coin.

In connecting with others we have the potential of being listened to, a place where we can tell the honest truth and therefore hopefully be freed from the tension that we feel and know that there are others who understand all that is going on in our lives. We find support here, comfort and companionship in the decisions that we make.

Try and deal with difficult people

Very few people find confrontation easy. For the vast majority of us it is the last thing we want to do and when we do have to confront someone the whole experience is physically and emotionally draining. And yet positive confrontation is a good coping skill when we are being made to suffer because of the actions of others.

A young man recently went to speak to a manager where he works. The manager had on several occasions made unreasonable requests of him and was regularly rude and

145

offensive. Although aware of some major problems in the manager's personal life, the employee felt she had no right to speak to him in the tone she used or make the demands that she did. Rather than let the issue escalate he decided to nip it in the bud. This took immense courage and you have to admire his guts – and his self-worth!

When it comes to expressing our concerns to someone, there are a few healthy tips to keep in mind.

- Focus on the issue and not the person. State the nature of the problem and how you feel.

- Next, encourage open discussion.

- Then, look to see the relationship develop rather than go backwards.

- After this, focus on positive ways forward and, if at all possible, help the other person to save face. Think win-win. Most people when they are confronted over their behaviour internally acknowledge that they have been stupid, so what you don't want to do is corner them so that they have no way out.

- You want to be appropriately assertive (consider taking a short course if necessary). You have every right to be heard and it would be good to give them self-respect as well.

Take time out

It doesn't really matter where you go or what you do, but a useful way of coping with stressful situations is to take time out. A tip offered by the Mayo Clinic website for those going away on a family holiday is to plan to regularly take fifteen-minute breaks of solitude. In their opinion it is long enough to restore your energy and motivation. It is pretty good advice for those going through any type of a tough time – though sometimes longer is better and necessary.

When one man found himself going through thirty-three hours of labour with his wife, one of the ways that he coped was to take a five-minute walk every hour. One friend finds picking up a book and reading a chapter very soul restoring. Another friend goes fishing for the morning, another watches an episode of *The Simpsons*. Next time at work when things become overwhelmingly stressful, if appropriate, what about taking a walk and finding a quiet place and giving yourself an opportunity to clear your mind, slow your breathing and bring calm to your inner being?

Give yourself a talking to

In the film *Vantage Point* we are told the story of how an American president was shot. This tragic tale is recalled for us from the perspective of eight strangers. Fascinatingly, each of them has a different take on what happened. It seems that there is far more to the event than any of them thought.

When it comes to the traumas, stresses and strains of life, many of us attempt a single definition of what is happening to us. We failed the exam because the teacher did not like us or the reason why we didn't get promotion was because we weren't related to the boss or the cause of our cancer is the fact that we are not very nice people and this is God punishing us.

A difficult coping discipline to master, but one well worth learning, is that of disputing your own thoughts – your initial thoughts. As is illustrated by the Psalms in the Old Testament, there is a place to give oneself a talking to;

to explore in our mind whether there is the possibility of an alternative take on what happened. We can consider whether there could be a different explanation rather than be buried by our own pessimistic thoughts.

So here is the ABCDE of self-talk. First, we need to identify what is the point of **adversity** – what exactly is the problem? Is it our boss being 'off' with us, the unreasonable hours we have been asked to work or the difficult colleague that we have been assigned?

Second, what are the negative **beliefs** that have been triggered by this adversity – is there a sense of rejection, mistreatment or lack of appreciation for our skills to be assigned such a poor colleague?

Third, we need to identify what the **consequences** are of finding ourselves in this scenario. Are we acting in a particular way or are there particular negative emotions that we are feeling?

Fourth, we need to **dispute** the negative beliefs. Could it be that the reason that the boss is 'off' with us has nothing to do with our performance but rather a relationship difficulty at home? Could it be that they are asking us to work long hours on this particular project because they know that we are highly committed to the company? Have we been paired with this seemingly incompetent colleague not because we too are viewed as weak but rather because it is recognized that we have the skills to train them and bring out the best in them?

The fifth component of this approach is then to focus on the more optimistic reasons for the problem and experience the **energizing** that that brings.

Martin Seligman points out that the key to this inner conversation is the quality of the argument that you have with yourself. Ultimately, you can't fool yourself and so it is important that you develop a strategy for having a meaty conversation in your own mind. How do you do that? You do it by playing detective.

To begin with we need to look for any evidence that may support our initial take on the situation. Next we need to find possible alternative explanations. Pessimists often latch on to the worst case scenario, which is usually void of any reality. Therefore it is important to scan the facts and identify which parts may be reinterpreted. Ask yourself what those alternatives could be. Following on from thinking about the positive alternatives we need to reconsider the implications. Challenge any negative beliefs that may have come from finding yourself in a difficult place. Lastly, weigh up the consequences of the ABCDE exercise and ask whether the outcome really is that bad. So what if our boss does not like us? There are other people he/she doesn't like too.

It is wise to have this type of conversation with yourself in an appropriate place – it may even be useful to have it on paper (but not too far from a shredder).

Think more positively

Closely connected with giving yourself a talking to is the coping option of looking at what positives could come out of the difficult period that you are presently going through. Now, let's be serious. Not every cloud has a silver lining. Sometimes you can go through a tragedy and there is nothing but devastation.

It would be an insult to glibly suggest that in every situation in which we find ourselves there were personal rewards to be gleaned. Where is the fruit of a daughter being raped or of thousands of lives being lost because of a tsunami? Who wins when the seas are polluted or a factory closes and workers find that they can't get another job?

With that said, some people do learn to thrive precisely because of the way they respond to hardship. This therefore provides a hope to latch on to as you go through your next 'end of the world as we know it' episode.

What are some of these A-list advantages? For some there is the feeling that one's life has great value or there is a change in life perspective. Others experience a sense of personal growth or a maturing of character; still others a deepening of their relationships or an appreciation of the preciousness of life. Every now and then there is a developing of a deeper and more sophisticated and satisfying philosophy of life – though that normally follows on from life's horrible moments that force us to ask some of the bigger questions of life.

It may not be our first route for personal growth, but there is no doubt that difficult experiences can be a health spa for personal renewal. Running deeply under this argument is a belief structure that causes us to find meaning in the darkest of places. We'll take a look at belief structure at the end of the chapter.

Get yourself ready

Time management makes a huge difference. It may prove to be difficult finding the time to manage your time, but for those who can take a moment to work on their schedule the rewards are huge. On some occasions, we are aware that we are entering a particularly stressful time. As we approach that point it helps to have conversations with family and friends about how things are going to be harder for a little while, to maybe schedule in specific non-negotiable occasions when you will be out of the office and out of reach. It is always a good idea to plan in some simple treats through the day and to hold the thought that life isn't always going to be like this.

Pray

Prayer enables us to tap into the divine life that fills the universe. In the older western tradition, this divine life is referred to as the God and father of Jesus. What that means is that if Jesus is anything to go by then God is going to be a good person to have around during those difficult moments. Most people pray in a crisis and Jesus reveals that the one to whom we pray can be trusted to be actively involved and near us at these times.

Learn to say no

Some of us love to say yes to people. We may be optimists at heart and want to see the best in everyone and everything brought out. It is easy under these circumstances to fill our diary several times over. But is saying yes always the best response? It is easier to say yes, but at what personal cost do we agree to something?

At the end of the day, it is about knowing your priorities and limitations. If you say yes then how is that going to affect your quality time with your family? Do you really have the time to give your best to this project? What about giving someone else an opportunity to be involved?

When it comes to making a decision, if possible it is always good to sleep on it. One of the ways you can stop yourself from being railroaded is by not taking your diary with you wherever you go and, if you do, be sure to have marked in your diary days off and free time and holidays. It is surprising how powerful it is to say, 'I'm sorry, but I can't do that as there is something already in my diary.'

Laugh

We believe in the power of laughter and are almost convinced of its miraculous powers. Such is the power of laughter that it can bring stress relief, improve immune systems and even relieve pain.

In addition to the above, there is also a place for learning to accept what you are going through, identifying the signs of stress in your life and what stress triggers you may have, ensuring that you get enough sleep and making sure that you get enough physical exercise.

A spiritual worldview and suffering

In the ancient manuscript of Ecclesiastes its author offers us two ways of looking at the world. He says that you can either look at life from 'under the sun' or you can look at life 'under heaven'.

To perceive life 'under the sun' is to see it within the parameters of birth and death. Reality is that which you can touch, see and reason. There is a spiritual dimension to life but it is more of a sixth sense or, as Freud would say, a sick-sense.

When it comes to seeing life 'under heaven' the idea presented is that of an open heaven where there is a mingling of the spiritual and the human. The parameters of life are not birth and death – as Frodo discovered as he caught the last ship to leave middle earth. Reality is not just what you can see, touch and reason; it also has a defined spiritual dimension – as Jodie Foster's character, Dr Eleanor Ann Arroway, discovered in the film *Contact* there is another aspect to this world, one that is more real and probably more powerful than the one we live in. Within this paradigm the God of the older western tradition is to be found.

Clearly there are many people who construct their lives around what we have called living 'under the sun'. Sonja Lyubomirsky observes:

When some people look at the world they see it as a place where there is a degree of controllability and predictability. I can to some extent determine my future and I have a rough idea of how things work. As part of this outlook are the ideas that bad things happen to bad people and good things happen to good people. It is a just world where things do not happen at random.

What happens when severe distress breaks into our lives is that we find our 'assumptive world', as psychologists call it, often shaken to the core. Why is this happening to me? How could God let this happen to me; haven't I been a good person?

This is a very traumatic experience for most people, as they are forced to consider that their belief structure does not hold water – it may be good in theory but it does not stand up in practice. What is more, there is the additional pain of having to re-configure their perspective on their identity and personal worth and of having to accept that there is no guaranteed future.

Since our beliefs determine how we see the world and react to life's events, the argument is that those who find meaning in suffering find it easier to cope.

We have found that having God in the picture brings us realistic hope, a source of courage and an awareness of his involvement in our lives. That does not mean that everything in this life makes sense or that we always get what we want or that all things in this life end well. But it does mean that we go through life knowing that God will care for us in many practical ways, that he will work all things for our good and that one day everything will make sense.

Conclusion

There is hope for Valerie and for the rest of us as we face up to or find ourselves living with the stresses and strains of life. We all suffer, and the journey out is not an easy one – honestly facing where you are in life and determining to make painful decisions is hard; learning to look at problems and not run away requires strength and skills. Life can be difficult – yet it is possible to experience a deeper happiness that is not dependent on present or outward circumstances.

Epilogue

In the blockbuster film *The Pursuit of Happyness* the formula presented is that true happiness is found in achieving financial security for yourself and your family. The film illustrates how the journey to taking hold of your pot of gold can be extremely difficult but once you have paid the price of realizing your dream then fulfilment seemingly awaits.

But is that really true? There clearly have been people who have amassed large sums of money and who have considerably improved the quality of their lives, but how many of them are happy – deeply happy? And what about the rest of us who will never have 'enough' or are dealt life cards which are unfair and difficult?

Within the pages of this book we have set out a rationale for a deeply happy life. We have shown that it is possible to wake up happy and that doing so is more a consequence than a purpose, more about how you live than what you accumulate, more about what is happening on the inside rather than the outside.

The pursuit of happiness demands that we consider making changes on the inside and that we recognize and respond to the reality that we are spiritual beings and that we learn to cultivate life habits that help the path of happiness.

As spiritual people living in a material world, we can discover how to live as such in the nitty gritty and highs and lows of daily life and thus increase the odds of enjoying deep, fulfilling happiness.

APPENDICES

Appendix 1: Saying Grace

General prayer for all occasions:

Thank you, God.

Before or at a family gathering

Father in heaven,
Bless us all as we gather here today [tonight]
And let us live happily in your love.
Amen.

At a wedding

Thank you for [name] and [name]. Help them to enjoy today and to deeply connect with each other.

Before food

Thank you for what we are about to receive and for those who made it for us. Amen.

Appendix 2: Joining a Group

One of the most popular and well-known groups is called Alpha. It has courses running all over the UK and USA. In fact, it is something of a global franchise. Information about Alpha can be obtained from visiting the website www.alpha.org.

A new course that has been written by Paul Griffiths is called 'Puzzling Questions'. Following the format of food, presentation and discussion it is an ideal six-week course for those who want to dip their toe in the water and engage with others in a non-threatening explorative environment with no expectation of any formal commitment to anything after the six weeks. Over the six sessions it looks at the six most popular spiritual questions being asked by people today. Information about this course can be obtained by visiting www.puzzlingquestions.org.uk.